LI PO VIEWING A WATERFALL

By a Japanese artist, Korin (1661–1716)

LI PO, THE CHINESE POET

李白詩集

小畑薫良譯

THE WORKS OF
L I · P O
THE CHINESE POET
DONE INTO ENGLISH VERSE BY
SHIGEYOSHI OBATA

With an Introduction and Biographical
and Critical Matter Translated
from the Chinese, together
with the Chinese Texts

PARAGON BOOK REPRINT CORP.
New York
1965

Library of Congress Catalog Card Number: 65-26103

An unaltered and unabridged reprint
of the work published in Tokyo 1935
Reprinted by Paragon Book Reprint Corp.

Printed in the United States of America

TO

MY FATHER

of Eighty years

From whom in my boyhood I learned
the old stories and great
classics of China

PREFACE

This is the first attempt ever made to deal with any single Chinese poet exclusively in one book for the purpose of introducing him to the English-speaking world.

Li Po has been the best-known Chinese poet in the Orient for the last one thousand years or more. In America his name has only recently been made familiar to the poetry public through the translation of his poems by eminent contemporary poets. But as the Bibliography at the end of the present volume indicates, Li Po—variously designated as Le Pih, Ly Pé, Li Tai-pé, Li Tai-po, *et cet.*—has been known more or less to Europe during the past century. A prominent place is accorded the poet in all the French and German anthologies of Chinese poems, which have appeared from time to time. He is included among the *Portraits des Célèbres Chinois* in Amiot's *Mémories* (1776–97), while Pavie's *Contes Chinois* (1839) has a *nouvelle* of his life. Excellent studies and translations have been made by two German scholars, Florenz and Bernhardi, in their monographs on the poet.

In the English language, there is Mr. Edkins' paper "On Li Tai-po," which was read before the Peking Oriental Society in 1888 and was published in that Society's Journal in 1890. Mr. Edkins was perhaps the first Englishman to pay special attention to our poet, though his translations are trite and barren. Professor Giles, *Chinese Poetry in English Verse* and *History of Chinese Literature* came out respectively in 1898 and 1901. While

[v]

his dexterous renderings of Li Po and other poets have since been generally accepted as standard English versions, they fail to create an appetite for more of their kind owing probably to the professor's glib and homely Victorian rhetoric which is not to the taste of the present day. Mr. Cranmer-Byng is elegant, but somewhat prolix. His two books, *A Lute of Jade* and *A Feast of Lanterns*, have many gorgeous lines, suffused, I fear, with a little too much of Mr. Cranmer-Byng's own impassioned poetry. These three men belong to the old school of translators, who usually employ rhyme and stanzaic forms.

Then, in 1915, Mr. Ezra Pound entered the field with his *Cathay*, a slender volume of a dozen or more poems mostly of Li Po, "translated from the notes of the late Professor Fenollosa and the decipherings of Professors Mori and Ariga." In spite of its small size and its extravagant errors the book possesses abundant color, freshness and poignancy, and is in spirit and style the first product of what may be called the new school of free-verse translators, who are much in evidence nowadays. I confess that it was Mr. Pound's little book that exasperated me and at the same time awakened me to the realization of new possibilities so that I began seriously to do translations myself. Mr. Waley omits Li Po from his first book, but includes in his *More Translations* a few specimens from a group of poems that he published in the *Asiatic Review*, in which he avers that he does not regard Li Po so highly as others do. On the other hand, Miss Lowell devotes her recent delightful volume, *Fir-Flower Tablets*, largely to our poet, with a selection of eighty-five poems by him. Mr. Bynner's translation of what he calls *Three Hundred Pearls of Tang Poetry*, has been announced for early publication, in which Li Po will be represented by some twenty-five poems.

Now to the Western literary world, generally speaking, much of Chinese poetry remains still an uncharted sea for adventure. The romantic explorer who comes home from it may tell any tale to the eager and credulous folk. Not that yarns are wilfully fabricated, but on these strange vasty waters, dimly illumined with knowledge, one may see things that are not there and may not see things that are really there. Such is certainly the case with Li Po. For instance, Mr. Edkins speaks of a poem (No. 72) which he entitles "A Japanese Lost at Sea," as being "unknown in China" but having been preserved by the Japanese. He adds with the pride of a discoverer that the poem was given him by a Japanese in 1888, whereas as a matter of fact the same poem has for these centuries had a place in any Chinese edition of Li Po's complete works. Take another example. Due to the devious and extremely hazardous nature of his method of translation, Mr. Pound gathers two different poems of Li Po into one, incorporating the title of the second piece in the body of his baffling conglomeration. Even Mr. Waley registers his fallibility by a curiously elaborate piece of mistranslation in the *Asiatic Review*. Speaking of Li Po's death, he quotes from Li Yang-ping's *Preface* a passage, rendering it as follows:

When he was about to hang up his cap (a euphemism for dying), Li Po was worried . . .

which should read, to follow Mr. Waley's manner,

When I was about to hang up my cap (a euphemism for resigning from office), Li Po was sick. . . .

Preface

"Kua Kuan," a quite common Chinese phrase, meaning to hang one's cap, that is, one's official cap, is never used as a conceit for dying. In her Introduction to *Fir-Flower Tablets*, Mrs. Ayscough is right in rejecting the tempting morsel of legend about Li Po's drowning, which has been accepted by Professor Giles and others. But on the same page she makes a misstatement to the effect that Li Po after his return from exile went to "live with his friend and disciple, Lu Yang-ping, in the mountains near Kiu Kiang." The fact is Li Yang-ping (not Lu Yang-ping) was then magistrate of Tang-tu, the present city of Tai-ping in the province of Anhwei, at a considerable distance from the Lu Mountains, which are in Kiangsi. Nor does she seem to be conversant with the notorious bit of China's literary history regarding the "Eight Immortals of the Winecup." They acquired their enviable fame in the taverns of Chang-an during Li Po's sojourn in that metropolis. Tu Fu's celebrated poem (No. 125) will serve as an evidence. The group never lived in the mountains together as Mrs. Ayscough makes out. Again she blunders glaringly and inexcusably in writing, "China's three greatest poets, Li Tai-po, Tu Fu, and Po Chu-i all lived during his (Ming Huang's) long reign of forty-five years," for elsewhere in her own book the years of these poets are correctly given to be respectively, A. D. 701–762, 712–770 and 772–846.

By citing these few obvious errors committed by zealous scholars and daring poets, I do not mean to discredit their brilliant achievements, which I fully appreciate, and to which I am heavily indebted in the execution of my work. Only I feel it my duty to indicate to my reader the still very imperfect state of what is accessible to him in the way of a Li Po literature in English. And conscious of my own failings, I offer him my book in all humility although I have profited by the contributions of my predecessors, and although I feel that in the limited scope I have chosen, my work is generally adequate.

I am a Japanese. I pretend to no erudition in Chinese literature. But I have been all my life a student and lover of Chinese poetry, or as much of it as I can read. In my boyhood I learned some shorter pieces of Li Po by heart. And during these past years of my study and travel in America I have always carried with me a small edition of his works. These translations were made at intervals, over half of them having been finished before the spring of 1916. It is more than a year since the entire collection was completed and I began to look for a publisher. A few of the poems were published in the *Wisconsin Literary Magazine,* a student publication at the University of Wisconsin where I did my graduate work in English during 1917–1918. One poem (No. 9) was printed by a friendly editor in 1919 in the now defunct *Art and Life.* All the rest is presented to the public for the first time.

For the historical and biographical matter in the *Introduction* I drew only on the most reliable Chinese sources such as the writings of the poet himself and his contemporaries and the two *Books of Tang,* while I referred constantly to the works of European historians and translators. As to the poems themselves, they represent only a little more than one-tenth of the works of Li Po preserved in the standard Chinese edition, but I have tried to make the selection as varied and representative as possible and included, consequently, a number of popular

pieces which have been translated by more than one hand.
I have honestly tried my best to follow the original poems
closely and to preserve the peculiar emotional color of
each poem, waiting for the moment when I was in the
right mood to take up a particular piece. For the eluci-
dation of the difficult passages I depended largely on
Japanese and Chinese commentaries, and consulted freely, wherever possible, existing European translations; and
I had also the assistance of my Chinese friends. But I
wish to have my reader understand that many of my versions are far from being literal. A literal translation
would often leave a Chinese poem unintelligible unless
supplied with a great amount of exegesis, and I did not
wish to empty all the rich content of the original into
footnotes. I have amplified or paraphrased on many oc-
casions. I have omitted unimportant words here and
there. I have discarded, or translated, a number of proper names because, some way or other, Chinese syllables
refuse to sing in company with English words. I have
dropped all the phonetic marks, which indicate some tonal
peculiarities in certain words like *T'ang yün*, *fêng*, etc.,
but which serve only to mystify a non-initiate like myself
or my reader. But after all these and other things I have
done, I am inclined to believe that my renderings are
often simpler and more exact than other extant versions,
which I have studied and which I have listed at the end
of the book.

In conclusion, I acknowledge my heavy obligations to
all my European and American precursors in the field
and to my many personal friends who have aided me in
various ways during these years of protracted toil. I
mention specially my Chinese friend, Mr. Yulan Fung,

who went over the entire manuscript and furnished me with valuable criticism and corrections, and also Mr. Lo and Mr. Yang who did for me the Chinese titles of the poems, which appear at the margins of the succeeding pages. Finally my deepest gratitude is due to my old friend, Arthur Harcourt Mountain, without whose enthusiastic interest and frequent companionship and collaboration this book might have never been brought to completion.

SHIGEYOSHI OBATA.

New York City.
February 3rd, 1922.

NOTE TO THE ORIENT EDITION

In preparing the present edition, although I have introduced a few minor changes into the text, I have resisted the temptation to make revisions for the purpose of forestalling the charge of inaccuracy that may be raised by the Oriental reader. I firmly believe that my methods of translation described in the preface are well-suited to a work of this kind, which is primarily intended not for scholarly exactitude but for poetic appreciation and enjoyment.

I wish to thank my friends and reviewers who have kindly pointed out the errors and misprints in the New York and London editions, which are all corrected in this book.

S. O.

Tokyo,
November 3rd, 1935.

CONTENTS

PART I—POEMS BY LI PO

INTRODUCTION   1

PAGE

1. ON THE SHIP OF SPICE-WOOD 27
2. A SUMMER DAY. 29
3. NOCTURNE 30
4. A FAREWELL SONG OF WHITE CLOUDS . 31
5. THE LONG-DEPARTED LOVER 32
6. LADY YANG KUEI-FEI AT THE IMPERIAL
   EEAST OF THE PEONY—I 33
7. LADY YANG KUEI-FEI AT THE IMPERIAL
   FEAST OF THE PEONY—II 34
8. LADY YANG KUEI-FEI AT THE IMPERIAL
   FEAST OF THE PEONY—III 35
9. A POEM COMPOSED AT THE IMPERIAL COM-
   MAND IN THE SPRING GARDEN, WHILE
   LOOKING ON THE NEWLY GREEN WIL-
   LOWS BY THE DRAGON POND AND LIS-
   TENING TO THE HUNDRED-FOLD NOTES
   OF THE FIRST NIGHTINGALES 36
10. TO HIS FRIEND DEPARTING FOR SHUH . 38
11. TO HIS THREE FRIENDS 39
12. ADDRESSED HUMOROUSLY TO TU FU . . 41
13. ON A PICTURE SCREEN 42
14. ON ASCENDING THE NORTH TOWER ONE
    AUTUMN DAY. 44
15. THE SUMMIT TEMPLE 45

Contents

		PAGE
16.	LAO-LAO TING, A TAVERN	46
17.	THE NIGHT OF SORROW	47
18.	THE SORROW OF THE JEWEL STAIRCASE	48
19.	THE GIRL OF PA SPEAKS	49
20.	THE WOMEN OF YUEH—I	50
21.	THE WOMEN OF YUEH—II	51
22.	THE WOMEN OF YUEH—III	52
23.	THE WOMEN OF YUEH—IV	53
24.	THE WOMEN OF YUEH—V	54
25.	THE SOLITUDE OF NIGHT	55
26.	THE MONUMENT OF TEARS	56
27.	ON A QUIET NIGHT	57
28.	THE BLUE WATER	58
29.	THE CHING-TING MOUNTAIN	59
30.	WITH A MAN OF LEISURE	60
31.	THE YO-MEI MOUNTAIN MOON	61
32.	ON THE CITY STREET	62
33.	ON THE DEATH OF THE GOOD BREWER OF HSUAN-CHENG	63
34.	TO HIS WIFE	64
35.	THE POET THINKS OF HIS OLD HOME	65
36.	SORROW OF THE LONG GATE PALACE—I	66
37.	SORROW OF THE LONG GATE PALACE—II	67
38.	AN ENCOUNTER IN THE FIELD	68
39.	TO WANG LUN	69
40.	ON SEEING OFF MENG HAO-JAN	70

PAGE

41. ON BEING ASKED WHO HE IS 72

42. IN THE MOUNTAINS 73

43. THE FAIR QUEEN OF WU 74

44. WHILE JOURNEYING 75

45. THE RUIN OF THE KU-SU PALACE . . . 76

46. THE RUIN OF THE CAPITAL OF YUEH . . 77

47. THE RIVER JOURNEY FROM WHITE KING CITY 78

48. BY THE GREAT WALL—I 79

49. BY THE GREAT WALL—II 80

50. THE IMPERIAL CONCUBINE 81

51. PARTING AT CHING-MEN 82

52. ON THE YO-YANG TOWER WITH HIS FRIEND, CHIA 83

53. AWAKENING FROM SLEEP ON A SPRING DAY 84

54. THREE WITH THE MOON AND HIS SHADOW 85

55. AN EXHORTATION 86

56. THE INTRUDER 88

57. THE CROWS AT NIGHTFALL 89

58. TO MENG HAO-JAN 90

59. TO TUNG TSAO-CHIU 91

60. TAKING LEAVE OF A FRIEND 96

61. MAID OF WU 97

62. THE LOTUS 98

63. TO HIS TWO CHILDREN 99

64. TO A FRIEND GOING HOME 101

Contents

		PAGE
65.	A Mountain Revelry	102
66.	The Old Dust	103
67.	A Pair of Swallows	104
68.	At a River Town	105
69.	I Am a Peach Tree	106
70.	The Silk Spinner	107
71.	Chuang Chou and the Butterfly	108
72.	The Poet Mourns His Japanese Friend	109
73.	In the Spring-time on the South Side of the Yangtze-kiang	110
74.	The Steep Road to Shuh	111
75.	Parting at a Tavern of Chin-ling	115
76.	The Phoenix Bird Tower	116
77.	His Dream of the Sky-land: A Farewell Poem	117
78.	In Memoriam	120
79.	On the Road of Ambition	121
80.	To Tu Fu from Sand Hill City	122
81.	A Vindication	123
82.	To Luh, the Registrar	124
83.	To the Fisherman	125
84.	The Tears of Banishment	126
85.	The Lotus Gatherer	127
86.	The Sport-Fellows	128
87.	The Dancing Girl	129
88.	The Rover of Chao	130

PAGE

89. TO HIS FRIEND AT CHIANG-HSIA . . . 132

90. THE CATARACT OF LUH SHAN—I . . . 134

91. THE CATARACT OF LUH SHAN—II . . . 135

92. BEREFT OF THEIR LOVE 136

93. LADY WANG CHAO KUN—I 138

94. LADY WANG CHAO-KUN—II 139

95. THE NORTH WIND 140

96. THE BORDERLAND MOON 142

97. THE NEFARIOUS WAR 143

98. BEFORE THE CASK OF WINE 144

99. YUAN TAN-CHIU OF THE EAST MOUNTAIN 145

100. LINES 146

101. THE BALLADS OF THE FOUR SEASONS—
SPRING 146

102. THE BALLADS OF THE FOUR SEASONS—
SUMMER 149

103. THE BALLADS OF THE FOUR SEASONS—
AUTUMN 150

104. THE BALLADS OF THE FOUR SEASONS—
WINTER 151

105. TWO LETTERS FROM CHANG-KAN—I . . 152

106. TWO LETTERS FROM CHANG-KAN—II . . 154

107. ON ASCENDING THE SIN-PING TOWER . . 156

108. ON GOING TO VISIT A TAOIST RECLUSE ON
MOUNT TAI-TIEN, BUT FAILING TO MEET
HIM 157

109. AT THE CELL OF AN ABSENT MOUNTAIN
PRIEST 158

Contents

PAGE

110. ON A MOONLIGHT NIGHT 159

111. A VISIT TO YUAN TAN-CHIU IN THE MOUNTAINS 160

112. A MIDNIGHT FAREWELL 161

113. THE SONG OF LUH SHAN 162

114. TO HIS WIFE ON HIS DEPARTURE—I . . 164

115. TO HIS WIFE ON HIS DEPARTURE—II . 165

116. TO HIS WIFE ON HIS DEPARTURE—III . 166

117. ON HIS WHITE HAIR 167

118. TO THE HONORABLE JUSTICE HSIN . . 168

119. ON HEARING THE FLUTE IN THE YELLOW CRANE HOUSE 169

120. ON HEARING THE FLUTE AT LO-CHENG ONE SPRING NIGHT 170

121. ON THE TUNG-TING LAKE—I 171

122. ON THE TUNG-TING LAKE—II 172

123. TO HIS WIFE 173

124. TO HIS FRIEND, WEI, THE GOOD GOVERNOR OF CHIANG-HSIA WRITTEN IN COMMEMORATION OF THE OLD FRIENDSHIP DURING THE DAYS OF HIS BANISHMENT AFTER THE TUMULT OF WAR . . 174

PART II—POEMS BY OTHER POETS CONCERNING LI PO   183

125. THE EIGHT IMMORTALS OF THE WINECUP 185

126. THE EX-MINISTER 187

127. A VISIT TO FAN WITH LI PO . . . 189

PAGE

128. PARTING WITH LI PO ON THE TUNG-TING
LAKE 190

129. AN INVITATION TO LI PO 191

130. TO LI PO ON A SPRING DAY 193

131. TO LI PO. 194

132. THE GRAVE OF LI PO 195

PART III—BIOGRAPHICAL NOTES ON LI PO
BY CHINESE AUTHORS   197

THE PREFACE TO THE FIRST EDITION OF
THE POETICAL WORKS OF LI TAI-PO . 199

LI PO—A BIOGRAPHY BY LI HSU . . . 204

LI PO—A BIOGRAPHY BY SUNG CHI . . 206

BIBLIOGRAPHY   211

NOTES ON CHINESE TEXTS 213

TRANSLATIONS AND WORKS ON LI PO . 215

POEMS OF LI PO TRANSLATED IN THIS
BOOK 219

PART I

INTRODUCTION

POEMS BY LI PO

INTRODUCTION

I

At the early dawn of medieval Europe China had reached the noontide of her civilization. Indeed, the three hundred years of the Tang dynasty beginning with the seventh century witnessed a most brilliant era of culture and refinement, unsurpassed in all the annals of the Middle Kingdom. And the greatest of all the artistic attainments of this period was in literature, and particularly in poetry. There were no dramatists; no romancers; but only poets—and poets there were galore.

"In this age," remarks a native critic, "whoever was a man, was a poet." And this is not satire. The "Anthology of the Tang Dynasty" consists of nine hundred Books and contains more than forty-eight thousand nine hundred poems by no less than two thousand three hundred poets. Moreover, since this collection was compiled as late as the eighteenth century by order of a Manchu emperor, it represents only a meager crop from a field that had suffered the ruthless ravages of time for fully a thousand years. Imagine, then, the vast efflorescence of what must have been veritably a tropic jungle of poesy!

Now a person may consider it no distinction to be counted one among these poets when the list is so large; but to be picked out as the greatest of them all—as the leader of this colossal army of immortals, is certainly a singular distinction and honor. And this honor falls to Li Po. He, by almost unanimous consent, is regarded as the greatest poet under the Tangs, and of China of all times. "He is the lofty peak of Tai," proclaims an admirer, "towering above ten thousand mountains and hills; he is the sun in whose presence a million stars of heaven lose their scintillating splendor."

Before attempting to follow the poet's career in detail, let us take a glance at China as it was under the Tang dynasty, especially under the famous emperor Hsuan Tsung, who was one time patron to Li Po, and whose long and illustrious reign, ending with his tragic fall, marks the golden age of Chinese poetry.

II

The Tangs came to power in the early decades of the seventh century when Mahomet was just starting out on his first campaigns. Tai Tsung, the second emperor of the dynasty, in the twenty-three years of his reign (627–650) consolidated the hostile sections of the country and laid a firm foundation for his empire, which he greatly expanded by conquering Tibet and subduing the Tartar tribes of the Mongolian desert. Wu Hu—an empress (684–704)—has been much maligned for usurping the male prerogative of sovereignty; but she was undoubtedly one of China's ablest rulers and did more than uphold the prestige of her land during the last quarter of the century. Then followed shortly Hsuan Tsung, who ascended the dragon throne in 713 and ruled for forty-two years.

It was an age of great political power for China. Her suzeraignty extended from Siberia to the Himalaya mountain range, and from Korea to the Caspian Sea. Tributes were paid by India and Tonkin. The Caliphs of Medina sent precious stones, horses, and spice. From the Japanese capital, Nara, came envoys and students at frequent intervals, while once, in 643, from far Greece Emperor Theodosius despatched a mission to the court of Cathay.

It was an age of prosperity. The fertile valleys of the Yellow River and the Yangtze-kiang were turned into fields of rice, barley and waving corn, amid gleaming streams and lakes. Peace reigned in China proper —the vast domain that had once been torn up and made desolate by internecine wars during the four centuries of the *Three Kingdoms* and the *Six Dynasties*. Even in the remotest rural district, the *wine-pennant*, a tavern sign, was seen flying on the roadside, denoting the presence of tranquillity and good cheer, while large cities like Lo-yang (i. e. Honan-fu, Honan) and Chin-ling (i. e. Nanking, Kiansu) flourished immensely with increasing trade and travel.

Chang-an, the present city of Hsian-fu in Shensi, was the capital and the wonder of the age. The city was never so rich, splendid, and spendthrift. "See ye," proudly sings a poet, "the splendor of the imperial abode, and know the majesty of the Son of Heaven!" Beside the main castle with its nine-fold gates, there were thirty-six imperial palaces that reared over the city their resplendent towers and pillars of gold, while innumerable mansions and villas of noblemen vied with one another in magnificence. By day the broad avenues were thronged with motley crowds of townfolk, gallants on horseback, and mandarin cars drawn by yokes of black oxen. And there were countless houses of pleasure, which opened their doors by night, and which abounded in song, dance, wine and pretty women with faces like the moon.

It was also an age of religious proselytism. Buddhism had been in China for centuries before the Tang dynasty, and the country was dotted with monasteries and pagodas. It was in the reign of Tai Tsung that Yuen Tsang, a Buddhist priest, made his famous pilgrimage to India and brought back several hundred volumes of Sanscrit sutras. While Confucianism remained ostensibly the guiding principle of state and social morality, Taoism had gathered a rich incrustation of mythology and superstition and was fast winning a following of both the court and the common people. Laotzu, the founder of the religion, was claimed by the reigning dynasty as its remote progenitor and was honored with an imperial title. In 636 the Nestorian missionaries were allowed to settle in Chang-an and erect their church. They were followed by Zoroastrians, and even Saracens who entered the Chinese capital with their sword in sheath.

Thus Chang-an became not only the center of religious proselytism, but also a great cosmopolitan city where Syrians, Arabs, Persians, Tartars, Tibetans, Koreans, Japanese and Tonkinese and other peoples of widely divergent races and faiths lived side by side, presenting a remarkable contrast to the ferocious religious and racial strife then prevailing in Europe. Again, in Chang-an there were colleges of various grades, beside special institutes for caligraphy, arithmetic and music. Astronomy was encouraged by Tai Tsung, who also filled the imperial library with more than two hundred thousand books. Hsuan Tsung saw to it that there was a school in every village in the fifteen provinces of his empire.

Hsuan Tsung himself was regarded as a perfect prince, wise and valiant, a sportsman accomplished in all knightly exercises and a master of all elegant arts. Being a musician, he established in his palace an operatic school, called the "Pear Garden," at which both male and female actors were trained, and in which historians find the prototype of the modern Chinese drama. The emperor surrounded himself with a brilliant court of poets, artists, and beautiful women. Odes were offered him by Li Po and Tu Fu; Li Kuei-nien sang at his bidding, while Yang Kuei-fei, the loveliest of the three thousand palace ladies, ever accompanied his palanquin. Although in his latter years he indulged in all sorts of extravagant revelry, he was never vulgar. It is fitting that he is still remembered by the name of *Ming Huang*—the "Illustrious Sovereign."

But in order to complete the picture of this era there is a darker side, which really brought into full play the spiritual energies of the Chinese race. Within, the court, from the very beginning of the dynasty, was upset more than once by the bloody intrigues of princes and princesses who coveted the imperial crown. Without, China had her Vandals and Goths and Franks, to whom her wealth and splendor offered irresistible temptation to pillage. The border warfare never ceased, and not without many a serious reverse for the imperial forces, which made forays in retaliation, often far into the hostile territories, losing their men by thousands. Tai Tsung's Korean expedition was nothing but a gigantic

[5]

fiasco, and the conquest of that peninsula was completed by generals of the Empress, Wu Hu. But in her reign the Kitans, a redoubtable foe, appeared on the northern border. In the west the restive and warlike Tibetans could not be wholly pacified by political marriages, in which the imperial princesses were bestowed on the barbarian chieftains from time to time. The armies of Hsuan Tsung were most unfortunate. In 751 thirty thousand men perished in the desert of Gobi; while in the campaigns in Yunnan against the southern barbarians the Chinese lost, it is said, two hundred thousand men. Finally came the rebellion of An Lu-shan, which like a storm swept the mid-imperial plains, drenched them in blood, and left the empire tottering on the brink of ruin.

An Lu-shan was a soldier of the Kitan race, who distinguished himself in fighting against his own tribes, and who won the favor of Yang Kuei-fei and the confidence of Hsuan Tsung. His promotion was rapid. He was ennobled as a duke, and made the governor of the border provinces of the north, where he held under command the best armies of the empire and nursed an inordinate ambition, biding his time. Meanwhile at the court, the blind love of Hsuan Tsung for Yang Kuei-fei was corrupting the government. Her brother Yang Kuo-chung was appointed prime-minister, while eunuchs held high offices of state. At last in the spring of 755, An Lu-shan, under the pretext of ridding the court of Yang Kuo-chung, raised the standard of rebellion. He quickly captured the city of Lo-yang, occupied the entire territory north of the Yellow River, comprising the provinces of Shansi and Chili, and was soon marching westward on Chang-an. He had proclaimed himself the Emperor of the Great Yen dynasty.

"Is it possible!" exclaimed Hsuan Tsung, now an aged monarch, in amazement at the ingratitude of his vassal and at the impending catastrophe. The defense at the Pass of Tung Kuan collapsed. The emperor was forced to flee from the capital one rainy morning, with his favorite mistress, and a handful of his faithful servants. The soldiers escorting Hsuan Tsung blamed Yang Kuo-chung for the disaster, and he and all his kin were massacred. Yang Kuei-fei herself did not escape. She was ruthlessly snatched from the arms of her imperial lover, and was strangled and buried on the roadside without ceremony. The emperor abdicated in favor of his son, and proceeded mournfully to Ssuchuan, the land of Shuh.

The new emperor, Su Tsung, mustered a strong army under General Kuo Tsu-i to oppose the foes. Confusion was added by the revolt of Prince Ling, the sixteenth son of Hsuan Tsung, who challenged the authority of his brother from his stronghold in the southern provinces, though this uprising was promptly suppressed. An Lu-shan was driven from Chang-an in 757, and was shortly murdered by his own son, who was in turn killed by An Lu-shan's general, Shi Ssu-ming, another Kitan Tartar, who assumed the imperial title and retained the northern provinces in his iron grip. But Shi Ssu-ming himself was soon assassinated by his son, and the rebellion came finally to an end in 762. We need not follow the history longer. In that very year the former emperor, Hsuan Tsung, who had returned from exile to a lonely palace in Chang-an, died, broken-hearted.

[7]

Such was the era. It had, on the one hand, internal peace, prosperity, cosmopolitan culture, profuse hospitalities and literary patronage; on the other, distant wars, court intrigues and, finally, the national catastrophe with its tragic drama of stupendous magnitude, that brought forth Li Po and his race of poets, kindled their imagination, and touched their heart-strings to immortal song.

III

The ancestry of Li Po is traced back through the obscurity of many generations to Li Kao of the fifth century, who ruled the Liang State, or the western portion of what is now the province of Kansu. The family dwelt in exile for a period in the Mongolian desert land. The poet himself writes of his being "Originally a cotten-clothed of Lunhsi." That is to say, he was a plain citizen of a district in Kansu. But he was born, according to best authorities, in the adjoining land of Shuh, or the present Ssuchuan—that picturesque western province of mountains and tumbling waters which flow into the great Yangtze-kiang.

As to the year of his birth, biographers again differ. Some maintain it to have been as early as 699, while others would have it as late as 705, with consequent variation in his age, since he died, as all agree, in the year 762. A biographical calendar, compiled by Sieh Chung-yung of the Sung dynasty, places the poet's birth in the second year of the Shen-lung era; while another calendar by Wang-chi of the Ching dynasty, who edited the complete works of Li Po, fixes the year as the first of the Chang-an era. All evidence seems to favor the latter date, which falls in the year of 701.

On the night of the poet's birth his mother dreamed of the planet of Chang-keng, which is Venus, and which is popularly known in China as the *Tai-po Hsing*, meaning literally the *Great White Star*. Thus it was that he was named Po (the *White* One), and surnamed Tai-po (the *Great White* One). Later he dubbed himself the Green Lotus Man, borrowing the name from a Bddhist saint; and sometimes went by the self-evident designation of the "Old Wine Genius."

When a boy of six Li Po could read, and by the age of ten he had mastered the Confucian books of the *Odes* and the *History* and miscellaneous classics by a hundred writers, and was composing poems of his own. While he was still in his teens, he retired with a recluse by the name of Tunyen-tzu to the mountain of Min in northern Ssuchuan. Here the two men kept strange birds as pets and succeeded in taming them to feed from their hands, the report of which brought to their hermitage the local magistrate, who invited them to enter the government service. But they declined. Our young poet sang contentedly:

> For twenty springs I've lain among the clouds,
> Loving leisure and enamored of the hills.

In 721 he traveled down the Yangtze to Yun-meng, the land of seven moors, that lies to the north of the river and the Tung-ting Lake; here he was married to a granddaughter of a certain ex-minister Hsu, and stayed there for three years.

Then he moved up north to Shantung, and made his home in Jen-cheng and elsewhere. "I am thirty," he wrote to a friend, "I make verses without tiring, while in front of my house carts and horses go by." Years passed without any visible achievement. One cannot blame too harshly his first wife who, impatient of the lack of his promotion, left him with the children. It was during this period that he became one of the "Six Idlers of the Bamboo Valley" who gathered in the mountain of Chu-lai for the jolly fellowship of wine and song. He traveled extensively, too. Once he was in the city of Lo-yang, enjoying the lavish hospitality of Tung Tsao-chiu, who had a special wine house built for the poet at the Tien-tsin bridge-head, where

> Songs were bought with yellow gold, and laughter with
> white jewels.[1]

Later the same host invited the poet to Ping-chou near Taiyuan-fu in Shansi, where Tung's father was stationed as the military commander. Here the two companions went on happy excursions, taking singing-girls out on the river by the dynastic shrine of Chin. It was in Ping-chou that the poet befriended Kuo Tsu-i, who was still a young soldier in the ranks, but who was later to become the savior of the empire as well as of the poet's life. In the year 738 Li Po was back in Shantung when Tu Fu, his one great and formidable rival in poetic fame, arrived in the province and met him. At once a warm friendship and exchange of poems began that lasted lifelong, and that makes the happiest and most

[1] See No. 59

memorable chapter in China's literary history. Tu Fu was the younger of the two. They slept together under one coverlet (so he tells us in one of his poems), and went hand in hand like two brothers.[2]

Li Po traveled south to the lands of Wu and Yueh of old to wander amid the ruins of once glorious palaces and among the lakes of lotus lilies, and chose to sojourn in a district called Yen, in Chehkiang, famous for the beauty of its hills and valleys. Here he met Wu Yun, scholar and Taoist, who on being summoned to court took Li Po with him to Chang-an, the capital of the empire.

It was about the year 742 that Li Po entered Chang-an, the golden metropolis, when the long prosperous years of the Tien-pao era had just begun, and the court of Hsuan Tsung had reached the pinacle of brilliance. Li Po went to see Ho Chi-chang, a guest of the crown prince, and showed his poems. The jovial courtier was so pleased that he bartered his gold ornament for wine and entertained the new-comer. Moreover, he commended the poet to the emperor. "I have in my house," he said, "probably the greatest poet that ever existed. I have not dared to speak of him to your Majesty because of his one defect, which is rather difficult to correct: he drinks, and drinks sometimes to excess. But his poems are beautiful. Judge them for yourself, sire!" So saying, he thrust in Hsuan Tsung's hand a bundle of manuscript. "Fetch me the author of these poems!" spoke the emperor instantly—so runs one story.

But according to other versions it was Wu Yun, or Princess Yu-chen, who introduced Li Po to the court.

[2] See No. 127

At any rate, the poet was given an audience in the Hall of Gold Bells. His discourse and ode at once won the admiration of the emperor, so that he feasted the poet at the Table of the Seven Jewels and assigned him to the Han-ling Academy. That is, Li Po was placed under imperial patronage, without any special duties but to write occasional poems, of which the ninth piece in the present book is an example.

He banqueted with lords and ladies in and out of the court, and sought frequently the taverns of the city. But who were his boon companions? A vivid portrayal of that much celebrated company, the "Eight Immortals of the Wine-cup," whose revels were the talk of Chang-an, is happily preserved for us in an equally celebrated poem by Tu Fu.

> *Chi-chang* rides his horse, but reels
>> As on a reeling ship.
> Should he, blear-eyed, tumble into a well,
>> He would lie in the bottom, fast asleep.
> *Ju-yang Prince* must have three jugfuls
>> Ere he goes up to court.
> How copiously his royal mouth waters
>> As a brewer's cart passes by!
> It's a pity, he mournfully admits,
>> That he is not the lord of Wine Spring.
> Our minister *Li* squanders at the rate
>> Of ten thousand *tsen* per day;
> He inhales like a great whale,
>> Gulping one hundred rivers;
> And with a cup in his hand insists,
>> He loves the *Sage* and avoids the Wise.

[12]

Tsung-chi a handsome youth, fastidious,
  Disdains the rabble,
But turns his gaze toward the blue heaven,
  Holding his beloved bowl.
Radiant is he like a tree of jade,
  That stands against the breeze.
Su Chin, the religious, cleanses his soul
  Before his painted Buddha.
But his long rites must needs be interrupted
  As oft he loves to go on a spree.
As for *Li Po,* give him a jugful,
  He will write one hundred poems.
He drowses in a wine-shop
  On a city street of Chang-an;
And though his sovereign calls,
  He will not board the imperial barge.
"Please your Majesty," says he,
  "I am a god of wine."
Chang Hsu is a caligrapher of renown,
  Three cups makes him the master.
He throws off his cap, baring his pate
  Unceremoniously before princes,
And wields his inspired brush, and lo!
  Wreaths of cloud roll on the paper.
Chao Sui, another immortal, elate
  After full five jugfuls,
Is eloquent of heroic speech—
  The wonder of all the feasting hall.

One day in spring Hsuan Tsung with Lady Yang
Kuei-fei held a royal feast in the Pavilion of Aloes.
The tree-peonies of the garden, newly imported from

India, were in full flower as if in rivalry of beauty with the emperor's voluptuous mistress. There were the musicians of the Pear Garden and the wine of grapes from Hsi-liang. Li Po was summoned, for only his art could capture for eternity the glory of the vanishing hours. But when brought to the imperial presence, the poet was drunk. Court attendants threw cold water on his face and handed him a writing brush. Whereupon he improvised those three beautiful songs[3] in rapturous praise of Yang Kuei-fei, which were sung by the famous vocalist, Li Kuei-nien, while the emperor himself played the tune on a flute of jade.

But it was one of these very songs,[4] according to a widely accepted tradition, that helped cut short the gay and prodigal career of the poet at the court. Kao Li-shih, the powerful eunuch, who had been greatly humiliated by having been ordered to pull off Li Po's shoes once as the latter became drunk at the palace, persuaded Yang Kuei-fei that the poet had intended a malicious satire in his poem by comparing her with Lady Flying Swallow, who was a famous court beauty of the Han dynasty, but who was unfaithful and never attained the rank of empress. This was enough to turn gratitude to venomous hate, and Yang Kuei-fei interfered whenever the emperor sought to appoint the poet to office. There is another tradition that Li Po incurred the displeasure of Hsuan Tsung through the intrigue of a fellow courtier. This story is also plausible. Li Po was not the sort of man fitted for the highly artificial life of the court, where extreme urbanity, tact and dissimulation, were

---

3 See No. 6, 7, & 8.
4 See No. 7

essential to success. He soon expressed a desire to return to the mountains; and the emperor presented him with a purse and allowed him to depart. He was then forty-five years old, and had sojourned in the capital for three years.

Once more Li Po took to the roads. He wandered about the country for ten years, "now sailing one thousand *li* in a day, now tarrying a whole year at a place, enjoying the beauty thereof." He went up northeast to Chinan-fu of Shantung to receive the Taoist diploma from the "high heavenly priest of Pei-hai." He journeyed south and met Tsui Tsung-chi, the handsome Immortal of the Wine-cup, who had been banished from the capital and was an official at the city of Nanking. The old friendship was renewed, and withal the glad old time. It is related that one moonlight night they took a river journey down the Yangtze from Tsai-hsi to Nanking, during which Li Po arrayed himself in palace robes and sat in the boat, laughing aloud, and rolling his frenzied eyes. Was it the laughter of wanton revelry, or of self-derision, or of haughty scorn at the foolish world that could not fathom his soul? In 754 Wei Hao, a young friend of his, came to meet him at Kuang-ling, Kiangsu Province, and traveled with him a while. To him Li Po entrusted a bundle of his poems, saying, "Pray remember your old man! Surely in the future I'll acquire a great fame."

Next year, in March of 755, we discover him fleeing from the city of Lo-yang amid the confusion of the war of An Lu-shan, whose troops occupied the city and made the waters of the Lo River flow crimson with blood. The poet went down to the province of Chehkiang, and final-

ly retired to the mountains of Luh near Kiu-kiang in
Kiangsi Province. When Li Ling, the Prince of Yung,
became the governor-general of the four provinces near
the mouth of the Yangtze, Li Po joined his staff. But
the subsequent revolt and the quick fall of the Prince in
757 lead to imprisonment of the poet at the city of Kiu-
kiang, with a sentence of death hanging over him. On
examination of the case officials were inclined to leniency.
One of them, Sung Ssu-jo, recommended the emperor not
only to pardon Li Po but to give him a high place in the
government service. But the memorial, which by the
way had been written by Li Po himself at Sung's direc-
tion, failed to reach its destination. Then Kuo Tsu-i,
now a popular hero with his brilliant war record, came
to the rescue; he petitioned that Li Po's life might be
ransomed with his own rank and title. The white head
of the poet was saved, and he was sentenced to perpetual
banishment at Yeh-lang—the extreme southwest region
of the empire roughly corresponding to by the present
province of Yunnan.

He proceeded westward up the river leisurely. There
seems to have been little pressure from the central government, certainly no inclination on the part of the poet,
to expedite the journey. At Wu-chang he was welcomed
by the local governor Wei, with whom he spent months
and climbed the Yellow Crane House three times. Further up he encountered Chia-chi, his former companion
at Chang-an, and Li Hua, a kinsman of his. These two
had also been demoted and dismissed from the capital.
The three luckless men now joined in a boat party more
than once on the Tung-ting Lake under the clear autumn
moon. That these were not so lugubrious affairs after

all is attested by their poems.[5]   After such delays and
digressions Li Po sailed up the Yangtze through the
Three Gorges and arrived in Wu-shan, Ssuchuan, in 759,
when amnesty was declared.

It was as if warmth enlivened the frozen vale,
And fire and flame had sprung from dead ashes.[6]

The old poet started homeward, resting a while at
Yo-chou and Chiang-hsia, and returning to Kiu-kiang
again. He visited Nanking once more in 761; and next
year went to live with his kinsman, Li Yang-ping, who
was magistrate of Tang-tu, the present city of Taiping
in Anhwei. Here in the same year he sickened and died.

A legend has it that Li Po was drowned in the river
near Tsai-shih as he attempted, while drunken, to em-
brace the reflection of the moon in the water. This was
further elaborated into a tale, which was translated by
Théodore Pavie. This story, quoted by d'Hervey Saint
Denys, is altogether too beautiful to omit. I retranslate
the passage from the French:

"The moon that night was shining like day. Li Tai-po
was supping on the river when all of a sudden there was
heard in the mid-air a concert of harmonious voices,
which sounded nearer and nearer to the boat. Then,
the water rose in a great tumult, and lo! there appeared
in front of Li Tai-po dolphins which stood on their tails,
waving their fins, and two children of immortality carry-
ing in their hands the banners to indicate the way. They
had come in behalf of the lord of the heavens to invite

[5] See No. 52, 121, 122, & 128.
[6] See No. 124

[17]

the poet to return and resume his place in the celestial realm. His companions on the boat saw the poet depart, sitting on the back of a dolphin while the harmonious voices guided the cortège. . . . Soon they vanished altogether in the mist."

As to Li Po's family and domestic life the curiosity of the western mind has to go unsatisfied. The Chinese biographers never bother about such trivialities of a man's private affairs. The Old and the New Books of Tang are both totally silent. Only in his preface to the collection of the poet's works Wei Hao remarks:

"Po first married a Hsu and had a daughter and a son, who was called the Boy of the Bright Moon. The daughter died after her marriage. Po also took to wife a Liu. The Liu was divorced, and he next was united to a woman of Luh, by whom he had a child, named Po-li. He finally married a Sung."

Hsu, Liu, and Sung are all family names of the women who were successively married to Li Po. Of his several poems extant, addressed to his "wife," it is difficult to tell just which one is meant in each case. From a poem[7] written to his children we learn that the girl's name was Ping-yang, and the son whom Wei Hao refers to by the unusual nickname of the "Boy of the Bright Moon," was called Po-chin. Of the third child, Po-li, mentioned by Wei Hao, there is no reference elsewhere. Po-chin died without having obtained any official appointment in 793.

---

[7] See No. 63

His one son wandered away from home; while his two daughters were married to peasants.

Although Li Po had expressed his desire of making the Green Hill at a short distance southeast of Taiping-fu his last resting place, he was buried at the "East Base" of the Dragon Hill. His kinsman, Li Hua, wrote the inscription on his tombstone. Twenty-nine years after the poet's death a governor of Tang-tu set up a monument. But by the second decade of the ninth century when another great poet, Po Chu-i, came to visit the grave, he found it in the grass of a fallow field. About the same time Fan Chuan-cheng, inspector of these districts, discovered the "burial mound three feet high, fast crumbling away"; he located the two granddaughters of Li Po among the peasantry, and on learning the true wish of the poet, removed the grave to the north side of the Green Hill and erected two monuments in January of 818.

IV

The Old Book of Tang says that Li Po "possessed a superior talent, a great and tameless spirit, and fantastical ways of the transcendent mind." In modern terminology he was a romanticist.

Like Wordsworth he sought the solitude of hills and lakes. But he was a lover rather than a worshipper of Nature. He was "enamored of the hills," he says. To him the cloud-girt peak of Luh Shan, or the hollow glen of autumn, was not a temple but a home where he felt most at ease and free to do as he pleased—where he drank, sang, slept, and meditated. He spent a large part of his life out of doors, on the roads, among the flowering trees, and under the stars, writing his innumerable poems, which are the spontaneous utterances of his soul, responding, to the song of a mango bird or to the call of far waterfalls. And his intimate Nature-feeling gained him admission to a world other than ours, of which he writes:

Why do I live among the green mountains?
I laugh and answer not. My soul is serene.
It dwells in another heaven and earth belonging to no
    man—
    The peach trees are in flower, and the water flows
    on. . . .

Taoism with its early doctrine of inaction and with its later fanciful superstitions of celestial realms, and supernatural beings and of death-conquering herbs and pellets fascinated the poet. Confucian critics, eager to whitewash him of any serious Taoistic contamination, declare that he was simply playing with the new-fangled heresy. But there is no doubt as to his earnestness. "At fifteen," he writes, "I sought gods and goblins." The older he grew, the stronger became the hold of Taoism on his mind. In fact, the utilitarian principle of Confucian ethics was alien both to his temperament and to the circumstances of his life. The first thing he did after his dismissal from the court was to go to Chi-nan-fu and receive the Taoist diploma from the high priest of the sect, "wishing only (says Li Yang-ping) to return east to Peng-lai and with the winged men ride to the Scarlet Hill of Immortality." Peng-lai is the paradisical land of the Taoist, somewhere in the eastern sea.

The poetry of Li Po reflects the gleams of such visionary worlds. His "Dream of the Sky-land," [8] rivaling *Kubla Khan* in its transcendent beauty and imaginative power, could not have been written but by Li Po, the Taoist. Even in superstition and opium there is more than a Confucian philosophy dreams of.

But mysticism and solitude filled only one half of the poet's life. For he loved dearly the town and tavern— so much so that he is censured again by moralists as having been sordid. Li Po not only took too hearty an interest in wine and women, but he was also scandalously frank in advertising his delight by singing their praise in sweet and alluring terms. In this respect Li Po, like so many of his associates, was a thorough Elizabethan. Had the Eight Immortals of the Wine-cup descended from their Chinese Elysium to the Mermaid Tavern, how happy they would have been with their doughty rivals in song, humor, wit, capacity for wine, and ardent and adventurous, if at times erratic, spirit!

Li Po "ate like a hungry tiger," says Wei Hao, who should know; while according to another authority, "his big voice could be heard in heaven." In his early youth he exhibited a swashbuckling propensity, took to errantry, and learned swordmanship, and even slashed several combatants with his cutlass.

"Though less than seven feet in height, I am strong enough to meet ten thousand men," he boasted. It is hardly necessary, however, to point out the rare and lovable personality of the poet, who made friends with everybody—lord or prince, Buddhist or Taoist, courtier or scholar, country gentleman or town brewer; and ad-

---

[8] See No. 77

dressed with the same affectionate regard alike the emperor in the palace and the poor singing-girl on the city street of Chang-an.

In his mature age Li Po, despite his natural inclination and temperament, cherished the normal Chinese ambition to serve the state in a high official capacity and try the empire-builder's art.[9] It was with no small anticipation that he went to the court and discoursed on the affairs of the government before the emperor. But he was only allowed to write poems and cover his vexations with the cloak of dissipation. Later when amid the turmoil of the civil war he was called to join the powerful Prince of Yung, his aspirations revived, only to be smothered in the bitterness of defeat and banishment. The last few years of his life were pathetic. Broken in spirit and weary with the burden of sorrow and age, but with his patriotic fervor still burning in his heart, he watched with anxiety the sorry plight of his country.

In the middle of the night I sigh four or five times,
Worrying ever over the great empire's affairs.

The rebellion of An Lu-shan and its aftermath were not wholly quelled till the very year of the poet's death.

Then, there was the inevitable pessimism of the old world. The thought of the evanescence of all temporal things brought him solace for life's disappointments, and at the same time subdued his great tameless spirit. The Chinese race was already old at Li Po's time, with a retrospect of milleniums on whose broad expanse the dynasties of successive ages were like bubbles. What Shake-

---

[9] See No. 79, & 124.

speare came to realize in his mellowed years about the "cloud-capt towers and gorgeous palaces," was an obsession that seized on Li Po early in life. Thus it is that a pensive mood pervades his poetry, and many of his Bacchanalian verses are tinged with melancholy. Even when he is singing exultantly at a banquet table, his suddest thought will out, saying "Hush, hush! All things pass with the waters of the east-flowing river."

POEMS BY LI PO

1. ON THE SHIP OF SPICE-WOOD

江上吟

My ship is built of spice-wood and has a rudder of *mu-lan;*
Musicians sit at the two ends with jeweled bamboo flutes
    and pipes of gold.
What a pleasure it is, with a cask of sweet wine
And singing girls beside me,
To drift on the water hither and thither with the waves!
I am happier than the fairy of the air, who rode on his
    yellow crane.
And free as the merman who followed the sea-gulls aim-
    lessly.
Now with the strokes of my inspired pen I shake the
    Five Mountains.
My poem is done, I laugh and my delight is vaster
    than the sea.
Oh, deathless poetry!   The songs of Chu-ping are ever
    glorious as the sun and moon,
While the palaces and towers of the Chu kings have
    vanished from the hills.
Yea, if worldly fame and riches were things to last for-
    ever,
The waters of the River Han would flow north-westward,
    too.

---

*The poet is in his typical mood.   The poem is a
manifesto of his happy triumphant existence of free-
dom and of sensual and poetical indulgence.*

Mu-lan is the name of a precious wood.

[27]

Chu-ping, or Chu Yuan, 332–295 B. C., was a loyal minister under Huai-wang, the ruler of the Chu state. He is celebrated for his poems, which include the famous Li Sao.

The river Han is a large tributary of the Yangtze, which originates in Shensi and flows southeastward through Hupeh, joining the main stream at Hankow.

2.   A SUMMER DAY

Naked I lie in the green forest of summer. . . .
Too lazy to wave my white feathered fan.
I hang my cap on a crag,
And bare my head to the wind that comes
Blowing through the pine trees.

3. NOCTURNE

秋
浦
歌

Blue water . . . a clear moon . . .
In the moonlight the white herons are flying.
Listen! Do you hear the girls who gather water-chest-
nuts?
They are going home in the night, singing.

4. A FAREWELL SONG OF WHITE CLOUDS

The white clouds float over the mountains of Chu—
As over the mountains of Chin.
Everywhere the white clouds will follow you on.

They will follow you on everywhere—
With you they will enter the Chu mountains,
And cross the waters of the Hsiang.

Yonder across the waters of the Hsiang,
There is a cloak of ivy to wear,
And you may lie in a bed of white clouds.

Go swiftly home, O my friend!

白雲歌送劉十六還山

5. THE LONG-DEPARTED LOVER

Fair one, when you were here, I filled the house with flowers.

Fair one, now you are gone—only an empty couch is left.

On the couch the embroidered quilt is rolled up; I cannot sleep.

It is three years since you went. The perfume you left behind haunts me still.

The perfume strays about me forever, but where are you, Beloved?

I sigh—the yellow leaves fall from the branch,

I weep—the dew twinkles white on the green mosses.

6. LADY YANG KUEI-FEI AT THE IMPERIAL FEAST OF THE PEONY—I

清
平
調
一

The glory of trailing clouds is in her garments,
And the radiance of a flower on her face.
O heavenly apparition, found only far above
On the top of the Mountain of Many Jewels,
Or in the fairy Palace of Crystal when the moon is up!
Yet I see her here in the earth's garden—
The spring wind softly sweeps the balustrade,
And the dew-drops glisten thickly. . . .

As to the occasion on which these songs were composed, see the Introduction.

The Mountain of Many Jewels is the abode of the fairy queen, Hsi-wang-mo; the Palace of Crystal is another such fabled home of beautiful spirits.

清
平
調
二

7. LADY YANG KUEI-FEI AT THE IMPERIAL FEAST OF THE PEONY—II

She is the flowering branch of the peony,
Richly-laden with honey-dew.
Hers is the charm of the vanished fairy,
That broke the heart of the dreamer king
In the old legend of the Cloud and Rain.
Pray, who in the palace of Han
Could be likened unto her,
Save Lady Flying Swallow, newly-dressed
In all her loveliness?

The Legend of Cloud and Rain: King Hsiang of Chu once in his dream saw a fairy maid whose loveliness captivated his heart instantly, and who, on being asked who she was, replied, "In the morning I am the cloud, in the evening the rain on the Wu mountains," and vanished. The amorous king pined for the cloud and rain, morning and evening ever after.

Chao Fei-yen or Lady Flying Swallow, was a singing girl of Chang-an, but her charm won the love of the emperor Cheng-ti of the Han dynasty, who took her up to the palace and made her an imperial concubine of the highest rank.   She is famous for her frail beauty.   It is said that she was of so slight a build that she could dance on the palm of the hand.   She lived in the 1st century B. C.

8. LADY YANG KUEI-FEI AT THE IMPERIAL FEAST OF THE PEONY—III

清
平
调
三

She stands, leaning against the balustrade
Of Chen-hsiang Ting, the Pavilion of Aloes.
Vanquished are the endless longings of Love
Borne into the heart on the wind of spring.
The radiant flower and the flowery queen rejoice together,
For the emperor deigns to watch them ever with a smile.

9. A POEM COMPOSED AT THE IMPERIAL COMMAND IN THE SPRING GARDEN, WHILE LOOKING ON THE NEWLY GREEN WILLOWS BY THE DRAGON POND AND LISTENING TO THE HUNDRED-FOLD NOTES OF THE FIRST NIGHTINGALES

The east wind blowing, the grass of Ying-chow is green;
The spring-sweetness is about the purple palaces and
crimson towers.
The willows on the south of the pond have turned half-
green,
They grow like delicate wreaths of mist
By the resplendent castle,
Their thread-like branches, one hundred feet long,
Dangling about the carved and painted pillars.
While high above the sweet birds sing melodiously to-
gether—
They sing with hearts stirred early by the spring wind,
Which rolls itself in the blue clouds and dies.

The voice of spring is heard all over—
By a thousand gateways and by ten thousand doorways.
At Hao-king, where my lord, the emperor, tarries,
Five colored clouds are brightening
Against the lucid purple of the sky.
The imperial cortege comes forth, agleam in the sun.
Coming forth from the golden palace,
The imperial car bedecked with jewels
Glides along the path of flowers,

[36]

First turning to the Peng-lai Garden,
Where cranes are seen gracefully dancing,
Then, returning to the garden of Yi-shih,
Where the first songs of nightingales are heard—
They sing high among the trees,
Desiring to mingle their notes with the mouth-organs,
And join the imperial concert of the phoenix-flutes.

Hao-king is an old name for Chang-an, the capital.

10. TO HIS FRIEND DEPARTING FOR SHUH

送
友
人
入
蜀

I hear the Tsan-tsung road
Is rough and rugged, and hard to travel.
It is so steep that the mountains rise
In front of the rider's face,
And the clouds gather about the horse's head.
But there you will find the plank-highway of Chin
Canopied in fragrant foliage,
And the sweet water of springtime
Flowing around the city wall of Shuh.
Go, my friend!   Our destiny's decided. . . .
You need not bother to ask Chuan-ping, the fortune-
   teller.

---

*Tsan-tsung is one of the mythical rulers of Shuh, or
the present Ssuchuan.*

*Chuan-ping was a fortune teller of Chengtu under the
Han dynasty.   As soon as he had earned a hundred
pence, he would close his shop and busy himself with
writing books.*

[38]

11.   TO HIS THREE FRIENDS

When the hunter sets traps only for rabbits,
Tigers and dragons are left uncaught.
Even so, men of blue-cloud ambition remain unsought,
Singing aloud at the door of their rocky den.

My friend, Han, you are rare and profound;
Pei, you possess a true clean breast;
And Kung, you, too, are an excellent man;
And all you three are lovers of cloud and mist.
Your stout and straight souls
Are loftier than the loftiest pine.
A flat boulder for a bed, you sleep together under one
        cover;
You hack the ice and sip water from the winter stream;
You own two pairs of shoes to wear among you three.

Once wandering as you please
Like the vagrant clouds,
You came out of the mountains to greet the governor.
Indifferently you wore cap and mantle a while,
Whistling long.

Last night you dreamed of returning to your old haunt,
And enjoying, you say, the moon of the Bamboo Valley.
This morning outside the east gate of Luh
We spread the tent and drink the farewell cup.

Be careful as you go!
The cliffs are snowy, and your horses may slip;

[39]

And the road of tangled vines may perplex you.
Pray remember,
My thoughts of longing are like the smoke grass,
That grows always in profusion, winter or spring!

The three friends were Han Chun, Pei Cheng, and Kung Chao-fu, all of whom were members of the "Six Idlers of the Bamboo Valley." These men were returning to the mountains after a brief and unsuccessful official career under the local governor, and Li Po wrote this parting poem.

12.   ADDRESSED HUMOROUSLY TO TU FU

Here! is this you on the top of Fan-kuo Mountain,
Wearing a huge hat in the noon-day sun?
How thin, how wretchedly thin, you have grown!
You must have been suffering from poetry again.

戲
贈
杜
甫

In contrast with Li Po, who depended largely on inspiration, Tu Fu was a painstaking artist careful of the minutest details.

観
元
丹
丘
坐
巫
山
屏
風

13. ON A PICTURE SCREEN

Whence these twelve peaks of Wu-shan!
Have they flown into the gorgeous screen
From heaven's one corner?

Ah, those lonely pines murmuring in the wind!
Those palaces of Yang-tai, hovering yonder—
Oh, the melancholy of it!—
Where the jeweled couch of the king
With brocade covers is desolate,—
His elfin maid voluptuously fair
Still haunting them in vain!

Here a few feet
Seem a thousand miles.
The craggy walls glisten blue and red,
A piece of dazzling embroidery.
How green those distant trees are
Round the river strait of Ching-men!
And those ships—they go on,
Floating on the waters of Pa.
The water sings over the rocks
Between countless hills
Of shining mist and lustrous grass.

How many years since these valley flowers bloomed
To smile in the sun?
And that man traveling on the river,
Hears he not for ages the monkeys screaming?

[42]

Whoever looks on this,
Loses himself in eternity;
And entering the sacred mountains of Sung,
He will dream among the resplendent clouds.

The screen was owned by his Buddhist friend, Yuan Tan-chiu, to whom Li Po has written innumerable poems. See No. 99.

The Wu-shan peaks are along the Yangtze gorges in Ssuchuan. The second stanza refers to the Legend of the Cloud and Rain. See the note under No. 7.

秋
登
宣
城
謝
朓
北
樓

14. ON ASCENDING THE NORTH TOWER ONE AUTUMN DAY

The waterside city stands as in a picture scroll.
The sky is lucid above the mountain shrouded in evening gloom,
While the waters on either hand shine like mirrors;
Two painted bridges span them like rainbows dropt from the sky.
The smoke from the cottages curls up around the citron trees,
And the hues of late autumn are on the green paulownias.
Who ever dreamed of my coming hither to the North Tower
To brood over the memory of Prince Hsieh, while the wind blows in my face?

The North Tower was built by Hsieh Tiao of the 5th century, a statesman and a poet of South Chi dynasty.
It is located in the city of Hsuan-cheng, Anhwei.

[44]

15.   THE SUMMIT TEMPLE

To-night I stay at the Summit Temple.
Here I could pluck the stars with my hand,
I dare not speak aloud in the silence,
For fear of disturbing the dwellers of heaven.

題峯頂寺

The temple is in a district in Hupeh, so isolated from the outside world that this poem of Li Po, written on a painted board and left on the beams of the ceiling, remained unmolested for centuries until it was discovered by a local magistrate, thus settling a dispute over its authorship which had arisen in the meantime, some attributing the poem to a certain Yang, who was born mute— the story runs—but on being taken to a high tower one day when he was only a boy of a few years, composed and uttered this poem, of which the first line reads:
"A precipitous tower, one hundred feet high!"

16. LAO-LAO TING, A TAVERN

勞
勞
亭

Here friends come, sorrowing, to say farewell,
O Lao-lao Ting, tavern where every heart must ache.
Here even the wind of spring knows the pain of parting,
And will not let the willow branches grow green.

---

*The tavern was situated on a hill-top just outside the
city of Nanking; and people seeing their friends off came
as far as this place to exchange parting cups.*

*The last line alludes to the Chinese custom of breaking
off a willow branch and presenting it to a departing friend.*

17. THE NIGHT OF SORROW

怨
情

A lovely woman rolls up
The delicate bamboo blind.
She sits deep within,
Twitching her moth eyebrows.
Who may it be
That grieves her heart?
On her face one sees
Only the wet traces of tears.

玉階怨 18. THE SORROW OF THE JEWEL STAIRCASE

The dew is white upon the staircase of jewels,
And wets her silken shoes. The night is far gone.
She turns within, lets fall the crystal curtain,
And gazes up at the autumn moon, shining through.

19. THE GIRL OF PA SPEAKS

巴
女
詞

The water of the River Pa is swift like an arrow;
The boat on the River Pa slips away
As if it had wings.
It will travel in ten days three thousand *li*.
And you are going, my dear—
Ah, how many years before you return?

Pa is the eastern region of Ssuchuan, traversed by the swift flowing Yangtze.

20. THE WOMEN OF YUEH—I

越
女
詞
一

She is a southern girl of Chang-kan Town;
Her face is prettier than star or moon,
And white like frost her feet in sandals—
She does not wear the crow-head covers.

---

*In these poems Li Po records what he saw of the
"southern" girls in Kiangsu and Chehkiang. These provinces were under the king of Yueh in the 5th and 6th
centuries, B. C.*

*Chang-kan is near the city of Nanking, and was at Li
Po's time inhabited by the lower class of people.*

*The crowhead covers are a kind of shoes worn by the
upper-class women of the north. So named on account
of their shape and very small size—small feet seem to
have been already at a premium. "It is interesting," remarks a native critic demurely, "to note Li Po's admiration for a barefoot woman."*

[50]

21. THE WOMEN OF YUEH—II

Many a girl of the south is white and lucent.
Often she will steer her shallop and play.
In her coquettish eyes
Lurks the lure of the spring-time.
She will pluck the flowers of the water
For amorous wayfarers.

22. THE WOMEN OF YUEH—III

越
女
词
三

She is gathering lotus in the river of Yeh.
She spies a passer-by, and turns round,
Singing her boat song.
She laughs, and hides away among the lilies;
And seeming shy, she will not show her face again.

23.   THE WOMEN OF YUEH—IV

She, a Tung-yang girl, stands barefoot on the bank,
He, a boatman of Kuei-chi, is in his boat.
The moon has not set.
They look at each other—broken-hearted.

越
女
詞
四

24. THE WOMEN OF YUEH—V

越
女
詞
五

The water of the Mirror Lake
Is clear like the moon.
The girl of Yeh-chi
Has a face white as snow.
Her silvery image
Trembles in the silvery ripple. . . .

25. THE SOLITUDE OF NIGHT

It was at a wine party—
I lay in a drowse, knowing it not.
The blown flowers fell and filled my lap.
When I arose, still drunken,
The birds had all gone to their nests,
And there remained but few of my comrades.
I went along the river—alone in the moonlight.

26. THE MONUMENT OF TEARS

The mountain of Hsien looks down on the Han River;
The water is blue and its sand shines like snow.
There on the mountain top stands the Monument of
    Tears.
Long weathered and covered up with green mosses.

The Mountain of Hsien is in Hupeh, near the city of Hsiang-yang. Once in the reign of the Chin dynasty (3rd century), Yang Hu, the governor of this district, a man of benevolence, climbed the mountain to view the fair landscape below. Amid the feasting and verse-making, the governor turned to his companions and said: "This mountain has stood here since the beginning of the world; and many famous men of virtue and wisdom have come up to this spot, as we ourselves. Now they are all gone and forgotten. Soon we shall be, too." So saying, he shed tears. Later the people erected a monument there. It is this that Li Po found "covered up with green mosses."

27. ON A QUIET NIGHT

I saw the moonlight before my couch,
And wondered if it were not the frost on the ground.
I raised my head and looked out on the mountain moon;
I bowed my head and thought of my far-off home.

静
夜
思

28. THE BLUE WATER

Blue is the water and clear the moon.
He is out on the South Lake,
Gathering white lilies.
The lotus flowers seem to whisper love,
And fill the boatman's heart with sadness.

29. THE CHING-TING MOUNTAIN

獨坐敬亭山

Flocks of birds have flown high and away;
A solitary drift of cloud, too, has gone, wandering on.
And I sit alone with the Ching-ting Peak, towering be-
    yond.
We never grow tired of each other, the mountain and I.

---

*The Ching-ting mountain is situated to the north of the
city of Hsuan-cheng, Anhwei.*

山中與幽人對酌

30. WITH A MAN OF LEISURE

Yonder the mountain flowers are out.
We drink together, you and I.
One more cup—one more cup—still one more cup!
Now I am drunk and drowsy, you had better go.
But come to-morrow morning, if you will, with the harp!

31. THE YO-MEI MOUNTAIN MOON

The autumn moon is half round above the Yo-mei
    Mountain;
Its pale light falls in and flows with the water of the
    Ping-chiang River.
To-night I leave Ching-chi of the limpid stream for the
    Three Canyons,
And glide down past Yu-chow, thinking of you whom
    I can not see.

峨
眉
山
月
之
歌

---

*This is one of the most famous poems in all Chinese
literature; and it is needless to say that the translation
does a gross injustice to the original verse, which com-
bines the beauty of a fluent language with the wealth of
charming associations that the proper names possess,
which, by the way, take up 12 of the 28 ideographs that
compose the whole poem.*

The mountain and stream are all located in Ssuchuan.

32. ON THE CITY STREET

相
逢
行

They meet in the pink dust of the city street.
He raises his gold crop high in salute.
"Lady," says he, "where do you live?"
"There are ten thousand houses among the drooping
　　willow trees."

33.   ON THE DEATH OF THE GOOD BREWER
OF HSUAN-CHENG

So, old man, you're down where the yellow waters flow.
Well, I imagine you are still brewing the "Old Spring-
time."
But since there's no Li Po on the Terrace of Night,
To what sort of people do you sell your wine?

---

*A Chinese tradition has it that in Hades there is a
spring, whose water is yellow. "The Yellow Spring" in
Chinese has long become a proper name, referring to the
world beyond.*

*"Terrace of Night" is another Chinese phrase for the
land of the dead.*

*"The Old Springtime," a brand of rice wine. The
Tang people named their rice wine frequently after the
season of spring. Tu Fu mentions a "Rice Spring."*

[63]

34. TO HIS WIFE

贈
内

Three hundred sixty days a year
Drunk I lie, like mud every day.
Though you're married to Tai-po, wife,
You might as well have been the Tai-chang's spouse.

*Tai-chang is the title of a religious officer in the gov-
ernment of the Han dynasty. Here a Tai-chang of the
latter Han dynasty is alluded to, who was noted for his
wine-bibbing propensity.*

35. THE POET THINKS OF HIS OLD HOME

I have not turned my steps toward the East Mountain
    for so long.
I wonder how many times the roses have bloomed
    there. . . .
The white clouds gather and scatter again like friends.
Who has a house there now to view the setting of the
    bright moon?

---

*The East Mountain (Tung Shan), in Chehkiang. Hsieh
An, the poet-governor of the 4th century under the Chin
dynasty, whom Li Po admired immensely, had resided
here.*

[65]

36. SORROW OF THE LONG GATE PALACE—I

The Northern Dipper has turned round in the sky,
And now hangs over the west tower.
In the Golden House there are none
Save the fireflies sailing the gloom,
While the moonlight falls
Into the Palace of Long Gate,
And deepens still more the sorrow of one in the secret
  bower.

---

*Lady Chen who was queen to Wu-ti, a Han emperor,
lost his favor and was left in the solitude of the Long
Palace Gate to pine alone.   Later at the imperial harem
of China, the "Sorrow of the Long Gate" became a stock-
phrase and served as a title for love poems of grief under
similar circumstances.*

The Northern Dipper, i. e. Ursa Major.

*The Golden House always refers to a palace for the
fair sex.*

37. SORROW OF THE LONG GATE PALACE—II 長門怨二

The glad spring goes unattended
At the laurel bower where sorrow is long;
But on the four walls of gold
The autumn dust clings like grief;
And night holds the bright mirror up in the emerald sky
For the lonely one in the Palace of Long Gate.

38.   AN ENCOUNTER IN THE FIELD

陌
上
贈
美
人

Came an amorous rider,
Trampling the fallen flowers of the road.
The dangling end of his crop
Brushes a passing carriage of five-colored clouds.
The jeweled curtain is raised,
A beautiful woman smiles within—
"That is my house," she whispers,
Pointing to a pink roof beyond.

39.　TO WANG LUN

贈汪倫

I was about to sail away in a junk,
When suddenly I heard
The sound of stamping and singing on the bank—
It was you and your friends come to bid me farewell.
The Peach Flower Lake is a thousand fathoms deep,
But it cannot compare, O Wang Lun
With the depth of your love for me.

The Peach Flower Lake is the name of the water as well as of the village on its shore.　Here Li Po spent some time, enjoying the hospitality of Wang Lun who had always a supply of good wine.　At the departure of the poet the host came out to the waterside to bid farewell in the manner described in the poem.

[69]

40. ON SEEING OFF MENG HAO-JAN

之黃
廣鶴
陵樓
　送
　孟
　浩
　然

My friend bade farewell at the Yellow Crane House,
And went down eastward to Willow Valley
Amid the flowers and mists of March.
The lonely sail in the distance
Vanished at last beyond the blue sky.
And I could see only the river
Flowing along the border of heaven.

---

*The Yellow Crane House stood till a recent date not far
from the city of Wu-chang, Hupeh, on a hill overlooking
the Yangtze-kiang.*

*Once upon a time a dead man of Shuh, traveling on
the back of a yellow crane, stopped here to rest. Hence
the name of the house.*

*There is another interesting story just as authentic, ac-
cording to which: there stood here a tavern kept by a man
whose name was Chin, to whom one day a tall rugged
professor in rags came and asked very complacently, "I
haven't money, will you give me wine?" The tavern
keeper was game; he readily offered to the stranger the
biggest tumbler and allowed him to help himself to all the
wine he wanted day after day for half a year. At last
the professor said to Chin, "I owe you some wine money.
I'll pay you now." So saying, he took lemon peels and
with it smeared on the wall a picture of a yellow crane,
which at the clapping of his hands came to life and danced
to the tune of his song. The spectacle soon brought a for-*

tune to the tavern-keeper; he became a millionaire. Then, the professor left, flying away on his bird, whither no one knew. The grateful tavern-keeper built the tower-house in commemoration thereof, and called it the Yellow Crane House.

Willow Valley (Yang-chow), in Kiangsu.

問白是何人　答湖州迦葉司馬

41.　ON BEING ASKED WHO HE IS

I call myself the Green Lotus Man;
I am a spirit exiled from the upper blue;
For thirty years I've hid my fame in wine shops.
Warrior of Lake Province, why must you ask about me?
Behold me, a reincarnation of the Buddha of Golden
　　　Grain!

---

*The Warrior of Lake Province happened to be a Bud-
dhist and the speaker of the assembly of his sect.　Hence,
Li Po's witticism in referring to the Buddhist theology.*

42.   IN THE MOUNTAINS

Why do I live among the green mountains?
I laugh and answer not, my soul is serene:
It dwells in another heaven and earth belonging to no
  man.
The peach trees are in flower, and the water flows
  on. . . .

43. THE FAIR QUEEN OF WU

口
號
吳
王
美
人
半
醉

The breeze passes through the lotus flowers—
All fragrance is the waterside pavilion.
The king of Wu is feasting on the Ku-su Tower.
Hsi-shih, the queen, flushed with wine, dances—
She is fair and unresisting.
Now, smiling, she leans near the east window
Against a couch of white jade.

---

*Hsi-shih (5th century B. C.) was queen to Fu Chai, the
king of Wu, and is one of the most famous court beauties
of China. Her dalliance cost the king his kingdom as
well as his life.*

[74]

44. WHILE JOURNEYING

The delicious wine of Lan-ling is of golden hue and
flavorous.
Come, fill my precious glass, and let it glow in amber!
If you can only make me drunk, mine host, it is enough;
No longer shall I know the sorrow of a strange land.

Lan-ling, in Shantung.

45. THE RUIN OF THE KU-SU PALACE

In the deserted garden among the crumbling walls
The willows show green again,
While the sweet notes of the water-nut song
Seem to lament the spring.
Nothing remains but the moon above the river—
The moon that once shone on the fair faces
That smiled in the king's palace of Wu.

---

*The Ku-su Palace is where King Fu-chai of Wu with
his beautiful queen Hsi-shih held perpetual revelries till
King Kou Chien of Yueh annihilated him. It was located
in the present city of Soo Chow, which was the capital of
Wu. See No. 43.*

46. THE RUIN OF THE CAPITAL
OF YUEH

Hither returned Kou Chien, the King of Yueh, in tri-
    umph;
He had destroyed the kingdom of Wu.
His loyal men came home in brilliance of brocade,
And the women of the court thronged the palace
Like flowers that fill the spring—
Now only a flock of partridges are flying in the twilight.

See Nos. 44 and 45.

[77]

47. THE RIVER JOURNEY FROM WHITE KING CITY

At dawn I left the walled city of White King,
Towering among the many colored clouds;
And came down stream in a day
One thousand *li* to Chiang-ling.
The screams of monkeys on either bank
Had scarcely ceased echoing in my ear
When my skiff had left behind it
Ten thousand ranges of hills.

*The White King City is in Ssuchuan, and Chiang-ling
in Hupeh. The distance between the two places is several
hundred miles, but the river flows so swiftly that the down
stream journey may be accomplished in a day.*

48. BY THE GREAT WALL—I

Came the barbarian horde with the autumn;
Out went the imperial army from the House of Han.
The general has divided the tiger tallies,
And the dunes of White Dragon are now
The camping ground of the brave.
The moon in the wilderness
Follows the movement of his bow,
And upon his sword the desert frost blossoms.
He has not even entered this side of the Jewel Gate Pass.
But do not heave a long sigh, O little wife!

---

*These poems tell the longing and the sorrow of young
wives, whose husbands are fighting the barbarians in a
distant land—a common theme for Tang poets.*

*The tiger tallies were used as a means of army regis-
tration. These were distributed among the soldiers prior
to their departure for the front, while the counterparts
were preserved at the headquarters.*

*The Jewel Gate Pass in western Kansu was located,
according to the old Chinese geography, 3600 li west of
Chang-an.*

49.   BY THE GREAT WALL—II

He rides his white charger by the Fortalice of Gold,
She wanders in dreams amid the desert cloud and sand.
It is a season of sorrow that she scarce can endure,
Thinking of her soldier lover at the border fort.
The fireflies, flitting about, swarm at her window,
While the moon slowly passes over her solitary bower.
The leaves of the green paulonia are tattered;
And the branches of the sha-tung blasted and sere.
There is not an hour but she, alone, unseen,
Weeps—only to learn how futile all her tears are.

50. THE IMPERIAL CONCUBINE

官中行樂詞

When a little child,
She was reared in a golden house,
Now ripe and lovely, she dwells
In the imperial palace of purple.
She will come forth from the innermost chamber,
A mountain flower in her glossy hair,
Robed in pink embroidered silk;
And always return at evening,
Accompanying the imperial palanquin.
Only, alas!—the hours of dance and song
Swiftly vanish into the sky
To tint, perhaps, the flying clouds in happy colors!

One of the eight poems entitled "Palace Pleasures,"
which Li Po composed during his sojourn at the court.
They describe the voluptuous life of Hsuan Tsung with
Yang Kuei-fei.

51. PARTING AT CHING-MEN

渡
荊
門
送
別

Faring far across the river-narrow of Ching-men
I have come with you into the land of Chu.
Here ends the mountain-range that stretches along the
　　plain,
While the river flowing on, enters the distant heavens.
Now under the moon like a mirror flying through the
　　sky,
And the rising clouds that build palaces and towers,
I bid you farewell.　Ten thousand *li* you sail away,
But it is the waters of the home river that bear you on.

52.   ON THE YO-YANG TOWER WITH HIS FRIEND, CHIA

与
夏
十
二
登
岳
陽
樓

Here from this tower we may view
The whole fair region of Yo-yang,
And the winding river
Opening into the Tung-ting Lake.

O wild geese, flying past,
Take away with you the sorrow of the heart!
And, come, thou mountain, give us thy happy moon!

Here will we sit to feast
And tarry a while with the clouds
And pass the cup high above the world of cares.

When we are goodly warm with wine,
Then, thou cooling breeze, arise!
Come and blow as we dance!
And our sleeves will flap like wings.

The Yo-yang Tower is situated in Yo-chou, Hunan province.

The poem was probably written while on his way to Yeh-lang, the place of his banishment. (*See Nos. 121 and 122*)

53. AWAKENING FROM SLEEP ON A SPRING DAY

春
日
醉
起
言
志

Life is an immense dream.　Why toil?
All day long I drowse with wine,
And lie by the post at the front door.
Awakening, I gaze upon the garden trees,
And, hark, a bird is singing among the flowers.
Pray, what season may this be?
Ah, the songster's a mango-bird,
Singing to the passing wind of spring.
I muse and muse myself to sadness,
Once more I pour my wine, and singing aloud,
Await the bright moonrise.
My song is ended—
What troubled my soul?—I remember not.

54. THREE WITH THE MOON AND HIS SHADOW

月
下
獨
酌

With a jar of wine I sit by the flowering trees.
I drink alone, and where are my friends?
Ah, the moon above looks down on me;
I call and lift my cup to his brightness.
And see, there goes my shadow before me.
Hoo! We're a party of three, I say,—
Though the poor moon can't drink,
And my shadow but dances around me,
We're all friends to-night,
The drinker, the moon and the shadow.
Let our revelry be meet for the spring time!

I sing, the wild moon wanders the sky.
I dance, my shadow goes tumbling about.
While we're awake, let us join in carousal;
Only sweet drunkenness shall ever part us.
Let us pledge a friendship no mortals know,
And often hail each other at evening
Far across the vast and vaporous space!

55. AN EXHORTATION

將
進
酒

Do you not see the waters of the Yellow River
Come flowing from the sky?
The swift stream pours into the sea and returns never-
more.
Do you not see high on yonder tower
A white-haired one sorrowing before his bright mirror?
In the morning those locks were like black silk,
In the evening they are all snow.
Let us, while we may, taste the old delights,
And leave not the gold cask of wine
To stand alone in the moonlight!

Gods have bestowed our genius on us;
They will also find its use some day.
Be not loath, therefore, to spend
Even a thousand gold pieces! Your money will come
back.
Kill the sheep, slay the ox, and carouse!
Truly you should drink three hundred cups in a round!

Come, Chin, my friend!
Dear Tan-chiu, too.
To you I offer wine, you must not refuse it.
Now I will sing a snatch of song. Lend ear and
hearken!
Little I prize gongs and drums and sweet-meats,
I desire only the long ecstasy of wine,
And desire not to awaken.

Since the days of old, the wise and the good
Have been left alone in their solitude,
While merry drinkers have achieved enviable fame.
The king of Chen would feast in ancient days
At his Palace of Peace and Pleasure;
Ten thousand measures of wine there were,
And reckless revelry forever.

Now let you and me buy wine to-day!
Why say we have not the price?
My horse spotted with five flowers,
My fur-coat worth a thousand pieces of gold,
These I will take out, and call my boy
To barter them for sweet wine.
And with you twain, let me forget
The sorrow of ten thousand ages!

56. THE INTRUDER

The grass of Yen is growing green and long
While in Chin the leafy mulberry branches hang low.
Even now while my longing heart is breaking,
Are you thinking, my dear, of coming back to me?
—O wind of spring, you are a stranger,
Why do you enter through the silken curtains of my
    bower?

57. THE CROWS AT NIGHTFALL

烏
夜
啼

In the twilight of yellow clouds
The crows seek their nests by the city wall.
The crows are flying home, cawing—
Cawing to one another in the tree-tops.
Lo, the maid of Chin-chuan at her loom
Weaving brocade,—for whom, I wonder?
She murmurs softly to herself
Behind the blue mist of gauze curtain.
She stops her shuttle, and broods sadly,
Remembering him who is far away—
She must lie alone in her bower at night,
And her tears fall like rain.

The theme of this poem is a well-known story of a young wife, who was left alone in Chang-an by her husband while he lived in another city with his mistress. The deserted wife composed poems of her love and fidelity, and weaving them into a piece of brocade, sent it to her husband, who was so moved thereby that he called her to his side and lived with her in happiness ever after.

Chin Chuan is an old name of Chang-an.

58. TO MENG HAO-JAN

贈
孟
浩
然

I like you, my friend, Meng,
Your love of beauty is something known
To everybody under heaven.
When young with red cheeks,
You cast aside your carriage and cap;
Now that your head is white,
You lie among the pine trees and the clouds.
You get drunk with the moon
As often as with the transparent wine;
And to the honor of serving the emperor
You prefer the rapture of blossoms.
Your nobility looms up like a high mountain,
Too high for others to attain to;
But they may breathe the rare fragrance
That your soul imparts.

---

*Meng Hao-jan was a native of Hupeh and a poet of no
mean reputation, ranking next to Li Po and Tu Fu in the
entire galaxy of the poets of the glorious Tang period.
He died in 740.*

59. TO TUNG TSAO-CHIU

Tung Tsao-chiu of Lo-yang, friend,
I remember the good old time.
You built me a wine house to the south of the Tien-chin
    Bridge
Songs were bought with yellow gold, and laughter with
    white jewels.
Months went by in one long lasting rapture; we scorned
    kings and princes.

Wise and valiant men from all shores were there as
    your guests.
Among them I was your special friend, you had my
    heart's devotion.
For you I would not have declined to uproot mountains
    and overturn the sea.
To you I bared my heart and soul without hesitation.

I journeyed to Hwai-nan to dwell in the laurel grove;
You remained in the north of Lo, with many sad dreams.
The separation was more than we could bear,
So we met again and went together.

We went together a long way to Hsien-cheng
Through the thirty-six turns of the river, winding round
    and round,
And amid the voices of the pine wind over the innu-
    merable cliffs,
Which having ceased—lo!

We burst into a valley—into the light of a thousand flowers.

There on the level ground with their horses of golden reins and silver saddles
Stood the governor of Han-tung and his men, who had come to meet us.
The Taoist initiates of Tzu-yang welcomed us, too, blowing on their jeweled bamboo pipes.
They took us on the Tower of Mist-Feasting,—what a music there stirred!
Such celestial notes! It seemed all the sacred birds of heaven sang together.
With those pipes playing, our long sleeves began to flap lightly.
At last the governor of Han-chung, drunken, rose and danced.
It was he, who covered me with his brocade robe;
And I, drunk too, chose his lap for pillow and went to sleep.
During the feast our spirits soared high over the ninth heaven,
But ere the morning we were scattered like stars and rain,
Scattered hither and thither, the Pass of Chu separating us wide,
As I sought my old nest in the mountains,
And you returned to your home across the Bridge of Wei.

Your honorable father brave as leopard and tiger
Became the governor of Ping-chow then.

And stopt the barbarian invasion.

In May you called me and I crossed the mountain of
Tai-hsing.

My cart wheels were broken on the steep passes, winding
like sheep guts; but that did not matter.

I traveled on and came to Pe-liang and stayed for months.

What hospitality! What squandering of money!

Red jade cups and rare dainty food on tables inlaid with
green jems!

You made me so rapturously drunk that I had no thought
of returning.

Oft we went out to the western edge of the city,

To the Temple of Chin, where the stream was clear as
emerald;

Where on a skiff afloat we played with water and made
music on pipes and drums;

Where the tiny waves looked like dragon-scales—and
how green were the reed in the shallows!

Pleasure-inspired, we took singing girls and gaily sailed
the stream up and down.

How beautiful are their vermilioned faces, when half-
drunken, they turn to the setting sun,

While the willow flakes are flying about them like snow,

And their green eyebrows are mirrored in the clear
water one hundred feet deep!

And comelier still are the green eyebrows when the new
moon shines.

The beautiful girls sing anew and dance in robes of thin
silk.

Their songs, lifted by the zephyr, pass away in the sky,
But the sweet notes seem to linger in the air, hovering
    about the wandering clouds.

The delight of those days cannot be had again.
I went west and offered my *Ode of the Long Willows,*
But to my skyey ambition the imperial gates were closed.
I came back to the East Mountain, white-headed.

I met you once more at the south end of the Bridge of
    Wei;
But once more we parted company north of Tsan-tai.
You ask me the measure of my sorrow—
Pray, watch the fast falling flowers at the going of spring!
I would speak, but speech could not utter all,
Nor is there an end to my heart's grief.
I call my boy and bid him kneel down and seal this letter,
And I send it to you a thousand miles, remembering.

---

*This poem was written shortly after Li Po's departure
from the capital, and tells of the companionship and excursions the poet had enjoyed with Tung Tsao-chiu before
his going to the court. He is now a disappointed man,
wandering over the country. See the* Introduction.

*Tung Tsao-chiu was a military official at Chiao dis-
trict in northern Anhwei not very far from the city of
Loyang.*

*Ping-chou, in central Shansi. The dynastic temple of
Chin is located near the city of Taiyuan-fu. This locality
was also called Pe-Liang.*

The Ode of the Long Willows was composed by the celebrated scholar and philosopher, Yang-Hsiung (B. C. 53—A. D. 18) of the Han dynasty. Here Li Po refers metaphorically to his own verse. The passage tells of his failure at the court.

60. TAKING LEAVE OF A FRIEND

Blue mountains lie beyond the north wall;
Round the city's eastern side flows the white water.
Here we part, friend, once forever.
You go ten thousand miles, drifting away
Like an unrooted water-grass.
Oh, the floating clouds and the thoughts of a wanderer!
Oh, the sunset and the longing of an old friend!
We ride away from each other, waving our hands,
While our horses neigh softly, softly. . . .

61. MAID OF WU

Wine of the grapes,
Goblets of gold—
And a pretty maid of Wu—
She comes on pony-back: she is fifteen.
Blue-painted eyebrows—
Shoes of pink brocade—
Inarticulate speech—
But she sings bewitchingly well.
So feasting at the table
Inlaid with tortoise shell,
She gets drunk in my lap.
Ah, child, what caresses
Behind lily-broidered curtains!

古
風

62. THE LOTUS

In the deep sequestered stream the lotus grows,
Blooming fresh and fair in the morning sun.
Its glowing petals hide the clear autumn water,
And its thick leaves spread like blue smoke.
Alas! in vain its beauty excels the world.
Who knows? Who will speak of its rare perfume?
Lo, the frost will come, chilling the air,
And its crimson must wither, its fragrance fade.
Ill it has chosen the place to plant its root.
Would it could move to the margin of a flower pond!

An obvious metaphor, reminding one of that flower which "wastes its sweetness in the desert air." Such poems were popular and accorded a high regard by the Chinese scholars, who relish greatly the moral meanings that they themselves read into the simple folk songs in the Book of Odes *compiled by Confucius. Li Po has left us a few scores of these allegorical poems, and it is these that Li Yang-ping in his* Preface *speaks of so highly. See Appendix II.*

63. TO HIS TWO CHILDREN

In the land of Wu the mulberry leaves are green,
And thrice the silkworms have gone to sleep.
In East Luh where my family stay,
I wonder who is sowing those fields of ours.
I cannot be back in time for the spring doings,
Yet I can help nothing, traveling on the river.
The south wind blowing wafts my homesick spirit
And carries it up to the front of our familiar tavern.
There I see a peach tree on the east side of the house
With thick leaves and branches waving in the blue mist.
It is the tree I planted before my parting three years
    ago.
The peach tree has grown now as tall as the tavern
    roof,
While I have wandered about without returning.
Ping-yang, my pretty daughter, I see you stand
By the peach tree and pluck a flowering branch.
You pluck the flowers, but I am not there—
How your tears flow like a stream of water!
My little son, Po-chin, grown up to your sister's shoul-
    ders,
You come out with her under the peach tree,
But who is there to pat you on the back?
When I think of these things, my senses fail,
And a sharp pain cuts my heart every day.
Now I tear off a piece of white silk to write this letter,
And send it to you with my love a long way up the river.

寄東魯二稚子

Written from Nanking during his southern travels prior to his journey to the court of Chang-an. His family lived in East Luh, a central part of Shantung.

64.   TO A FRIEND GOING HOME

It is June when the south wind blows the white sand,
And the oxen pant under the moon, their gusty breath
    turning to mist.
The lowland air is humid and suffocating, and it is hard
    to bear.
There is no coach on the long road in the burning heat.
What do you think of going by way of the river?
You leave for Chin-ling, hoisting your sail high to the
    breeze.
Your parents are waiting and watching for you, leaning
    against the gate.
In Luh-chung there is the home of your childhood.

My family live for the time at the Sand Hill;
I have not returned for three years, and they are dis-
    tracted.
Please, go and see them!—You know Po-chin, my boy.
He must be running his toy cart and riding on the back
    of a white sheep.

Written about the same time as No. 63.
*The poet is near Chin-ling—that is, Nanking.   In this
southern region the oxen are so afraid of the scorching sun
that they pant, it is said, even at the sight of the moon.*
*Luh-chung is a district, and Sand Hill a town, in
Shantung.   See No. 80.*

[101]

65. A MOUNTAIN REVELRY

To wash and rinse our souls of their age-old sorrows,
We drained a hundred jugs of wine.
A splendid night it was. . . .
In the clear moonlight we were loath to go to bed,
But at last drunkenness overtook us;
And we laid ourselves down on the empty mountain,
The earth for pillow, and the great heaven for coverlet.

66. THE OLD DUST

擬
古

The living is a passing traveler;
The dead, a man come home.
One brief journey betwixt heaven and earth,
Then, alas! we are the same old dust of ten thousand
    ages.
The rabbit in the moon pounds the medicine in vain;
Fu-sang, the tree of immortality, has crumbled to kin-
    dling wood.
Man dies, his white bones are dumb without a word
When the green pines feel the coming of the spring.
Looking back, I sigh; looking before, I sigh again.
What is there to prize in the life's vaporous glory?

_According to Chinese folklore there is a rabbit in the
moon, which is pounding the elixir of life._

67. A PAIR OF SWALLOWS

Swallows, two by two,—always two by two.
A pair of swallows are an envy for man.
Such a pair lived together once in a jeweled palace-tower.
Long they lived together by the gilded window with
    silken curtains.

Then fire swept the royal tower.
The swallows entered the Palace of Wu and made their
    nest.
But once more fire burned the palace down.
Burned away the swallow nest and all the younglings.
Only did the mother bird escape death; she is worn with
    grief.
Poor lonely swallow, she longs for her mate that is dead.
Never again, can the two fly together.
And that pierces my little heart with sadness.

---

*Another allegorical poem. A commentator says that
this is a fable of Li Po's own life, he with his hopes and
ambitions being compared with the mother swallow with
her mate and younglings. The first palace, then, would
allude to the court of Hsuan Tsung; and the second palace
to that of the Prince of Yung.*

68.   AT A RIVER TOWN

A river town.   The autumn rain has stopt.
Our wine is gone.   So, farewell!
While you lie idle in your boat,
Your sail flies down homeward over the waves,
Past the islands burning red with flowers,
Past the slender willows, green on the river strand.

What of me after parting?   I know not—
I'll go back, perhaps, to my old fishing rock on the beach.

69. I AM A PEACH TREE

I am a peach tree blossoming in a deep pit.
Who is there I may turn to and smile?
You are the moon up in the far sky;
Passing, you looked down on me an hour; then went on
    forever.

A sword with the keenest edge,
Could not cut the stream of water in twain
So that it would cease to flow.
My thought is like the stream; and flows and follows you
    on forever.

---

*These two stanzas are taken from a poem written by
Li Po in behalf of his wife, expressing her sentiment toward himself.*

70.   THE SILK SPINNER

Up the river by the White King City,
The water swells and the wind is high.
It is May.   Through the Chu-tang gorge
Who dares to sail down to me now—
Down to Ching-chow, where the barley is ripe
And the silk worms have made their cocoons—
Where I sit and spin, with my thoughts of you
Endless as the silken strands?
The cuckoo calls high up in the air.   Ah, me! . . .

荆
州
歌

---

*The White King City is in Ssuchuan.   The Chu-tang
gorge, situated near Wushan in the same province, is one
of the most dangerous spots in the Yangtze-kiang.   Further down the river and in Hupeh, Ching-chow is located,
where the silk spinner awaits her lover.*

71. CHUANG CHOU AND THE BUTTERFLY

Chuang Chou in dream became a butterfly,
And the butterfly became Chuang Chou at waking.
Which was the real—the butterfly or the man?
Who can tell the end of the endless changes of things?
The water that flows into the depth of the distant sea
Returns anon to the shallows of a transparent stream.
The man, raising melons outside the green gate of the
    city,
Was once the Prince of the East Hill.
So must rank and riches vanish.
You know it, still you toil and toil,—what for?

Chuang Chou.   *A famous philosopher of the 3rd and
4th centuries B. C., who was an ardent follower of Laotzu, the founder of Taoism. Chuang Chou's writing contains a chapter on his becoming a butterfly in a dream.*

72. THE POET MOURNS HIS JAPANESE FRIEND

哭晁卿行

Alas, Chao of Nippon—you who left the Imperial City
To sail the waters where the fabled islands are!
Alas, the bright moon has sunk into the blue sea never-
    more to return,
And gray clouds of sorrow fill the far skies of the south.

---

*Chao is the Chinese name adopted by a Japanese, Abe
Nakamaro, who, on arriving from Japan, was so fascinated with the brilliant court and city of Chang-an, that
he chose to remain in China all his life.   Once he sailed
for home, but his ship encountered a storm and was blown
to the south coast of China.   At the first report of the
mishap his friends at Chang-an believed that he was dead,
and threnodies were composed, of which this poem by Li
Po was one.*

73. IN THE SPRING-TIME ON THE SOUTH SIDE OF THE YANGTZE-KIANG

The green spring—and what time?
The yellow bird sings and will not cease.
On the bank of the Kiang I am growing old, white-haired.
My homeward way lies lost beyond the horizon.
Though my thoughts fly into the clouds of Chin,
I remain with my shadow under the moon of Chu.
My life is a wasted thing,
My garden and fields have long been buried under weeds.
What am I to do so late in my years
But sing away and let alone the imperial gate of gold?

74. THE STEEP ROAD TO SHUH

Alas! how precipitous! Alas! how high!
The road to Shuh is more difficult to climb than to climb
     the steep blue heaven.
In the remotest time of Tsang-tsung and Yu-fu—
Yea, forty milleniums ago—that land was founded.
Yet from the wall of the Middle Kingdom runs no high-
     way thither, no highway linking human dwellings;
Only a lone precipitous path—the bird-way—was built,
Leading westward toward the evening star,
And trailing across the forehead of the Yo-mei moun-
     tain.
And how those strong men died, traveling over!
The earth sunk and the mountains crumbled.
At last there is now a road of many ladders and bridges
     hooked together in the air.
Lo, the road-mark high above, where the six dragons
     circle the sun!
Lo, the stream far below, winding forth and winding
     back, breaks into foam!
The yellow crane could not fly over these mountain-
     tops;
And the monkeys wail, unable to leap over these gorges.
How the Green Mud path turns round and round!—
     There are nine turns to each hundred steps.
The traveler must climb into the very realm of stars, and
     gasp for breath;
Then draw a long sigh, his hands on his breast.

[111]

Oh, why go you west, I pray? And when will you return?

I fear for you. You cannot clamber over these jutting rocks.

You shall see nothing by day but the birds plaining bitterly on the aged trees, the female following the male in their flight;

You shall hear no voice but the cuckoos calling in the moonlight by night, calling mournfully in the desolate mountains.

The road to Shuh is more difficult to climb than to climb the steep blue heaven.

A mere story of it makes the youth's red face grow pale.

The lofty peaks shoot up cloudward in rows. If one foot higher, they would touch the heaven.

The dead pine trees cling to the cliff, hanging head down over the abyss.

The sparkling cascades and the spurting torrents vie with one another to make the bellowing din.

Anon, a giant boulder tumbles from the crag-head; a thousand mountain walls resound like thunder.

O you wayfarers from afar, why do you come hither on this direful road?

The gate of the Sword Parapet stands firm on its frightful height.

One man defending it, a thousand men could not break it open.

And the keepers of the gate are not of your kin,

They may turn, I fear, to wolves and leopards.

Fleeing at morn before the savage tigers,

Fleeing at eve before the huge serpents,
Men are killed and cut up like hemp,
While the beasts whet their fangs and lick the blood.
Though many pleasures there may be in the brocade city
    of Shuh,
It were better to return to your house quickly.
The road to Shuh is more difficult to climb than to climb
    the steep blue heaven.
I shrug my shoulders and heave a long sigh—gazing
    into the west.

This is one of the most admired and most difficult poems of Li Po, certain portions of it being as vague as they are beautiful. Some commentators maintain that this was written at the time of the An Lu-shan rebellion, when the emperor Hsuan Tsung fled to Ssuchuan, to which course Li Po was opposed; but being in no position to declare his opinion openly, the poet voiced it thus in verse covertly. The poem hints at the double danger for the emperor in leaving his capital to the rebels who are tigers and serpents as well as in trusting his person to the hands of the strangers of Shuh, who might turn to wolves and leopards, while it dwells for the most part on the difficulty of the journey in a remarkably vivid and forceful language. The Road to Shuh runs from Shensi to Ssuchuan over the mountains.

As to those "strong men" that died, there is this story: Some thousands of years ago, a prince in Shensi, knowing the fondness for women of the king of Shuh, offered him his five daughters for wives. The king despatched five strong men to fetch the princesses. It was on their homeward journey that the party saw a big serpent crawling into a hole in the mountainside. One man tried to pull out the serpent by its tail, but could not do so. All the five men joined in the enterprise, and yelling aloud, they pulled the serpent, whereupon the whole mountain range crumbled and was split into five peaks. The five strong men and the five princesses and all the attendants perished.

75.   PARTING AT A TAVERN OF CHIN-LING

The wind blows the willow bloom and fills the whole
    tavern with fragrance
While the pretty girls of Wu bid us taste the new wine.
My good comrades of Chin-ling, hither you have come
    to see me off.
I, going, still tarry; and we drain our cups evermore.
Pray ask the river, which is the longer of the two—
Its east-flowing stream, or the thoughts of ours at parting!

76.   THE PHOENIX BIRD TOWER

Here once on the Phoenix Bird Tower the phoenix birds
    came to nest.
Now the birds are gone, and the tower empty; only the
    river flows aimlessly on.
Here where the garden of Wu palace bloomed, the deep
    grass hides the paths;
Where the kings of Chin vaunted their regalia, is only
    an old hill.
I see the three peaks hang aloft as though half-dropt
    from the sky,
And the river divide in two streams, holding the White
    Heron Island between.
But the floating clouds cover the sun,
And the city of Chang-an is lost in distance and gloom.

---

*The Phoenix Bird Tower was situated to the north of
Nanking, once the capital of Wu, Chin, and many other
states. A legend has it that three birds of five-colored
wings, resembling the peacock, nestled here once, and they
sang so melodiously that all other birds of the vicinity
were attracted to the tower. Those three birds were the
Phoenix.*

77. HIS DREAM OF THE SKY-LAND: A FAREWELL POEM

夢遊天姥吟留別

The seafarers tell of the Eastern Isle of Bliss,
It is lost in a wilderness of misty sea waves.

But the Sky-land of the south, the Yueh-landers say,
May be seen through cracks of the glimmering cloud.

This land of the sky stretches across the leagues of
    heaven;
It rises above the Five Mountains and towers over the
    Scarlet Castle,
While, as if staggering before it, the Tien-tai Peak
Of forty-eight thousand feet leans toward the southeast.

So, longing to dream of the southlands of Wu and Yueh,
I flew across the Mirror Lake one night under the moon.

The moon in the lake followed my flight,
Followed me to the town of Yen-chi.
Here still stands the mansion of Prince Hsieh.
I saw the green waters curl and heard the monkeys'
    shrill cries.
I climbed, putting on the clogs of the prince,
Skyward on a ladder of clouds,
And half-way up from the sky-wall I saw the morning
    sun,
And heard the heaven's cock crowing in the mid-air.

[117]

Now among a thousand precipices my way wound round
    and round;
Flowers choked the path; I leaned against a rock; I
    swooned.

Roaring bears and howling dragons roused me—Oh,
    the clamorous waters of the rapids!
I trembled in the deep forest, and shuddered at the over-
    hanging crags, one heaped upon another.
Clouds on clouds gathered above, threatening rain;
The waters gushed below, breaking into mist.

A peal of blasting thunder!
The mountains crumbled.
The stone gate of the hollow heaven
Opened wide, revealing
A vasty realm of azure without bottom,
Sun and moon shining together on gold and silver palaces.

Clad in rainbow and riding on the wind,
The ladies of the air descended like flower-flakes;
The faery lords trooping in, they were thick as hemp-
    stalks in the fields.

Phoenix birds circled their cars, and panthers played
    upon harps.
Bewilderment filled me, and terror seized on my heart.
I lifted myself in amazement, and alas!
I woke and found my bed and pillow—
Gone was the radiant world of gossamer.

So with all pleasures of life.
All things pass with the east-flowing water.

I leave you and go—when shall I return?
Let the white roe feed at will among the green crags,
Let me ride and visit the lovely mountains!
How can I stoop obsequiously and serve the mighty ones!
It stifles my soul.

*In this poem the poet describes his dream of visiting
Mt. Tien-mu, "Fostermother of the skies," in Chehkiang.
The other mountains, Chi-Cheng, the "Scarlet Castle,"
and Tien-tai, the "Terrace of Heaven" are located in the
same province.*

Prince Hsieh is the one poet-governor mentioned in 35.

對
酒
憶
賀
監

78. IN MEMORIAM

(The poet mourns Ho Chi-chang)

Ssu-ming had a man of madness,
Ho Chi-chang, frenzied with wind and stream.
The first time I met him at Chang-an,
He called me "a god in exile."
O dear lover of the cup,
He has turned to sod under the pine tree—
He who bartered his gold turtle for wine.
Now, alone, I shed tears, remembering him.

---

*Ho Chi-chang. The jovial courtier who introduced Li
Po to Hsuan Tsung. Ssu-ming, a district in Cheh-kiang,
was his ancestral home, to which he retired and where he
died. See the Introduction, also No. 125.*

*The gold turtle was probably a trinket of some sort,
worn as an ornament.*

79.   ON THE ROAD OF AMBITION

(The poet departs from Nan-ling for the capital)

Home in the mountains in autumn-tide
Of new-brewed wine and yellow chick fattened on grain.
I call the boy to boil the fowl and pour the white wine,
While my children, playing noisily about, tug me by the
    sleeve.
I sing and imbibe the bland ecstasy of the cup;
I rise and dance in the tangled beams of the setting sun.

It is not too late to win a lord of ten thousand chariots.
Let me ride and spur my horse on the long, long road!

The silly woman of Kuei-chi may scorn Chu Mai-chen,
I take leave of my family and journey west to Chin.
Looking up at the sky, I laugh aloud and go.
Ha, am I one to crawl ever in the dust-laden weeds?

---

*Chu Mai-chen. Died B. C. 116. A wood-cutter under
the Han dynasty, whose wife left him because she could
not endure poverty. By diligent study, however, he became
governor of Kuei-chi in Chehkiang; and his wife, who had
sunk to destitution, begged to be allowed to rejoin him.
But he replied, "If you can pick up spilt water, you may
return"; whereupon his wife went and hanged herself—
Giles: Biographical Dictionary No. 65.*

*It is quite likely that the poet by the "silly woman of
Kuei-chi" alludes to his own wife, who had left him because
of his poor success in life.*

80. TO TU FU FROM SAND HILL CITY

沙丘城下寄杜甫

Why have I come hither, after all?
Solitude is my lot at Sand Hill City.
There are old trees by the city wall,
And busy voices of autumn, day and night.
The Luh wine will not soothe my soul,
Nor the touching songs of Chi move me;
But all my thoughts flow on to you
With the waters of the Min endlessly southward.

81.   A VINDICATION

If heaven loved not the wine,
A Wine Star would not be in heaven;
If earth loved not the wine,
The Wine Spring would not be on the earth.
Since heaven and earth love the wine,
Need a tippling mortal be ashamed?
The transparent wine, I hear,
Has the soothing virtue of a sage,
While the turgid is rich, they say,
As the fertile mind of the wise.
Both the sage and the wise were drinkers,
Why seek for peers among gods and goblins?
Three cups open the grand door to bliss;
Take a jugful, the universe is yours.
Such is the rapture of the wine,
That the sober shall never inherit.

月
下
獨
酌

82. TO LUH, THE REGISTRAR

贈靈司戶

It is autumn near and far.
Outside the gate all the hills are barren.
A white cloud, my old friend,
Beckons me from far empyreal space.
Pray, when will Luh Chen-ho come back—
He who has flown west like a crane?

A native commentator remarks: "*This poem would be better if the last two lines and the title were left out.*"

83. TO THE FISHERMAN

Shake not your crown, if perfumed;
Nor flap your garment, if spiced with *lan!*
It is better to hide the chaste soul's radiance,
The world hates a thing too pure.

There goes the fisherman of Tsang-lang.
Await me, old man, I will go with you.

84. THE TEARS OF BANISHMENT

The flow-tide ebbs back to sea.
My friend returned to Wu from banishment.
I asked him about the sorrows of exile.
His tears fell like pearls of the South Sea.

85. THE LOTUS GATHERER

採
蓮
曲

On the river margin of Jo-yeh she is gathering the lotus;
She talks to her companions and laughs among the lilies.
The clear sunlit water reflects her gay attire,
And her perfumed sleeves flap lightly in the wind.

But who are these cavaliers on the bank?
By twos, by threes, they glint through the drooping
    willows;
Their horses neigh among the blown flowers, and are
    gone.
She sees and lingers with an anguish in her heart.

---

*The Jo-yeh River is in Chehkiang, and flows into Ching
Hu, or the Mirror Lake.*

86.   THE SPORT-FELLOWS

君
馬
黄

You had a yellow steed,
Mine was white.
Their colors differed,
Our hearts were one.

We two gay blades of Lo-yang,
Rode the city street, side by side,
Flaunting our high head-gears gallantly,
Our long swords glancing in the sun.
Each had a fur coat on, worth a thousand guilders;
Both were guests of the five princes.

Now you have fallen as a tiger falls in a trap-hole;
And suffer miserably as strong men must sometimes.
But when you, my comrade, are so distressed,
What avails me if I alone can flourish?

87.   THE DANCING GIRL

With her limpid voice,
Her pearly teeth revealing,
The northern maid, the prettiest child,
Sings "Downy grasses," instead of "Blue water."
Then, brushing her face with her long sleeve, she rises
    for your sake.

She dances like the winter-cloud that curls over the
    frothy sea;
She dances like the wild fowl of Tartary, wind-blown
    toward the sky.

The kingly hall is full of radiant faces; the pleasure will
    not end.
With sundown the flute sounds thicken, and the mellow
    voices of the singing girls.

88. THE ROVER OF CHAO

侠
客
行

Oh, the Rover of Chao with his Tartar-fashioned cap,
A scimitar on his side, gleaming bright like the snow,
The silver saddle glittering on his white horse,
Behold, he comes and is gone like a shooting star;

Kills a man at every ten paces as he goes,
And goes he a thousand miles without stopping.
The deed done, he shakes his raiment and departs—
None knows whither, nor even his name.

He stops at leisure and drinks with Prince Hsin-ling,
Laying his drawn sword across his knee;
Picks up a piece of roast meat for Chu-hai to eat;
Offers a goblet of wine to Hou-ying to drink;

After three rounds gives a pledge of fealty,
And weightier is his vow even than the Five Mountains.
When his ears are hot and his eyes burn,
His heroic soul blazes forth like a rainbow.

A hammer in his hand saved the kingdom of Chao,
And the whole city of Han-tan shook with terror.
How the glory of two such strong men shines
For a thousand autumns over the ramparts of Tai-Liang!

Sweet honor perfumes their heroic bones,
Putting to shame the literati of the world,

[130]

Who can only recline in the study
And whiten their heads over books like the Tai-hsuan
    Ching.

Wu Chi was the name of Prince Hsin-ling of the Wei state in the 3rd century B. C.

Hou Ying was a recluse through whom Prince Hsin-ling obtained the service of Chu Hai, who was a rover of the type depicted in the present poem. When the state of Chao was attacked by a hostile state and its capital Han-tan was beleaguered, Hsin-ling and Chu Hai went to the rescue. Chu Hai—a very strong man—brained an irreso-lute general with a heavy hammer, while, by taking com-mand of his army, Hsin-ling raised the siege of Han-tan.

Tai-liang was the capital of the State of Wei.

Tai-hsuan Ching. A learned book written by Yang Hsiung (B. C. 53–A. D. 18).

89. TO HIS FRIEND AT CHIANG-HSIA

When the brazen Tartars came with their frightened
    horses kicking up dust and sand,
While the Tartar horde watered their horses in the Tien-
    chin River,
You, governor of Chang-yeh, then, resided near Wine
    Spring;
I, banished nine thousand *li*, was in the land of Pa.

When the world was put to order, and the laws made
    lenient,
I, an Yeh-lang exile, stricken with the chilly frost,
How I longed for my friend in the west whom I could
    not see.
Only the east wind bore my dream back to Chang-an.

What a chance that I met you in this place!
In joy and bewilderment I felt like one fallen from the
    cloud.
And amid the noise of pipes and flutes at the joyous feast
I endeavored in vain to utter long sentences.

Yesterday, clad in a brocade robe, I poured the costly
    wine.
To-day, sore-afflicted, I am dumb like the speechless
    trees.
Once I rode on horseback in the great imperial park;
Now I jog about slowly from house to house of man-
    darins.

At Nan-ping I met the governor to whom I bared my heart;
Now with you I may hold sweet conversation.
Even as the leagues of cloud melt above the mountain,
Opening the view of the blue sky around, so melts my
     grief.

Oh, grief! Oh, bitter pain, and pain evermore!
Sorrowing, I drink two thousand jugs of wine—
The cold ashes are warm again, and the spring is born.
And you, jolly wise host without compare,
Drunken, you go about, riding on the back of a mule.

In the cloister yonder under clouds and the moon there
     are monks galore.
But the mountains and waters—did they ever cater to
     man's desires?
Ah, no! Better blow your reed pipes, beat your drums,
     and wanton on the river water.
Call forth the young girls of the south and bid them
     sing the boat songs!

I will knock down the Yellow Crane House for you with
     a hammer,
You may upset the Parrot Island, too, for my sake.
The heroic battle of the Red Walls was fought as in a
     dream—
Let me sing and dance and lighten the sorrow of sep-
     aration!

望廬山瀑布水一

90. THE CATARACT OF LUH SHAN—I

Westward I ascend the Peak of Incense Burner;
Southward I see the mighty waterfall.
It plunges three hundred *chang* down the mountain,
And froths for miles in the rapids below.
As wind-driven snow speed the waters,
Like a white rainbow spanning the dark.
I wonder if Heaven's River had fallen from above
To course through the mid-sky of clouds.
Long I lift my gaze—Oh, prodigious force!
How majestic the creation of gods!
Unwavering before the ocean winds that blow,
Glaring at the faint moon from over the river,
   Profusely it sprays the sky
  And drenches the green mountain walls.
The swift torrents boil over giant rocks;
The flying water scatters a mist of ethereal gems.

O mountains of renown that I adore,
You fill my heart with deep repose.
No longer need I take the potion of precious stones,
You can wash away the earth stains from my face.
Let me be with the things I love,
And leave the world of man forever.

91. THE CATARACT OF LUH SHAN—II

The sun shines on the Peak of Incense Burner,
And the purple vapor rises like smoke.
Lo, the long stream of water hung up yonder!
Straight down three thousand *chi* the flying torrent leaps,
As if the Silver River were falling from the ninth heaven.

望廬山瀑布水二

The Silver River, i. e., The Milky Way.

92. BEREFT OF THEIR LOVE

遠
別
離

Bereft of their love,
Huang and Yin, the royal ladies of old,
Ranged the banks of Hsiao and Hsiang, south of Tung-
ting.
They wandered by the fathomless waters of the deep.
All the world tells the tale of their misery.
Dark is the day, and dismal the clouds;
Demons howl in the fog and infernal spirits whistle in
the rain.
Ah, me! What would it avail me if I dared to speak?
High heaven shines not, I fear, on the loyalty of my
heart.
Clouds gather clouds,—they would roar aloud in anger.
Even Yao and Shun ruling, the scepter would pass to
Yui.
A king, deprived of his minister, is a dragon turned to
a fish;
A minister usurps power, lo! a mouse is become a tiger.

Yao was imprisoned, they say, and Shun died in the
open field.
The Nine Hills of Perplexity stand in a row, one resembling another—
How could they find the solitary mound of the Double-
pupiled One?

The king's daughters cried where the black clouds
lowered;

Their lord was gone like wind and wave never to return.
They wept and moaned, and gazed into the distance.
Gazed longingly toward the deep mountains of Tsang-wu.

The Mountains of Tsang-wu may crumble, the River
    Hsiang go dry.
Their tears on the bamboo leaves will not fade forever.

*Huang and Hu Yin (24th century B. C.) were two
daughters of Emperor Yao, who gave them in marriage
to his successor, Shun—the Double-pupiled One. Shun,
while traveling south in the district of Tsang-wu (Hunan
Province) died and was buried in the field. The two
wives arrived too late to meet their husband, and their tear-
marks produced a new species of bamboo with speckled
leaves. Yui succeeded Shun as emperor.*

*The original of this poem, much prized for its verbal
beauty and its classic allegory, is quite obscure. The native commentators have a great deal to say on the significance of the second stanza. At any rate, it is clear that
Li Po, while retelling the well-known legend, alludes to
his separation from the emperor and to the unhappy state
of affairs at the court that was infested with unworthy
and wicked men.*

93. LADY WANG CHAO-KUN—I

王
昭
君
一

Lady Chao-kun brushes the saddle inlaid with pearl;
She mounts her palfrey and weeps,
Wetting her rose-red cheeks with tears.
To-day a high-born lady in the palace of Han,
To-morrow in a far land
She will be a barbarian slave.

Lady Wang Chao-kun, a lady in the seraglio of the emperor Yuan-ti of the Han dynasty, was one of the early victims of the political marriages, which the ruling house of China was compelled to make from time to time with the chieftains of the barbarian tribes in order to avoid their savage incursions into the Middle Flower Kingdom.

This emperor had so many beauties, it is said, that for the sake of convenience he ordered their portraits to be painted. All the ladies bribed the artist, except Lady Wang, who was consequently very unfavorably represented in the private gallery of the sovereign. So when a lady of the palace had to be presented to a Tartar chieftain, the emperor chose Wang Chao-kun, believing her to be the easiest one to spare. He discovered his mistake too late. She died in the barbarian land; singularly enough, over her little mound in the desert the grass, they say, was always green.

[138]

94. LADY WANG CHAO-KUN—II

王
昭
君
二

The moon above the palace of Han
    And above the land of Chin,
Shedding a flood of silvery light,
    Bids the radiant lady farewell.
She sets out on the road of the Jewel Gate—
    The road she will not travel back.
The moon returns above the palace of Han,
    Rising from the eastern seas,
But the radiant lady wed in the west,
    She will return nevermore.
On the Mongolian mountains flowers are made
    Of the long winter's snow.
The moth-eyebrowed one, broken-hearted,
    Lies buried in the desert sand.
Living, she lacked the gold,
    And her portrait was distorted;
Dying she leaves a green mound,
    Which moves all the world to pity.

95. THE NORTH WIND

北
風
行

The lamp-bearing dragon nestles over the polar gate,
And his light illumines the frigid zone.
For neither the sun nor the moon shines there,
But only the north wind comes, blowing and howling
    from heaven.
The snow-flakes of the Yen mountains are big like pil-
    lows,
They are blown down, myriads together, over the Hsuan-
    yuan palace.

'Tis December. Lo, the pensive maid of Yu-chow!
She will not sing, she will not smile; her moth-eyebrows
    are disheveled.
She stands by the gate and watches the wayfarers
    pass,
Remembering him who snatched his sword and went to
    save the borderland,
Him who suffered bitterly in the cold beyond the Great
    Wall,
Him who fell in the battle and will never come
    back.

In the tiger-striped gold case he left for her keeping
There remains a pair of white-feathered arrows
Amid the cobwebs and dust gathered of long years—
Oh, empty tokens of love, too sad to look upon!
She takes them out and burns them to ashes.

By building a dam one may stop the flow of the Yellow
River,
But who can assuage the grief of her heart when it
snows and the north wind blows?

96. THE BORDERLAND MOON

The bright moon is above the Peak of Heaven
In the far cloud-sea of Tartary.

The wind sweeps on for ten thousand miles
And blows over the Pass of the Jewel Gate.

The imperial army marches down the Po-tung road
While the barbarian foe peers into the Bay of Chin-hai.

The warriors watch the skies of the borderland,
And many faces are sad with thoughts of home.

Never yet from the battlefield
A man was seen returning—alas!

To-night at the high house, where she is waiting,
There is sighing and moaning without ceasing.

The Jewel Gate Pass, or Yu-men, in Anhsi, Kansu.
Po-tung. Perhaps, Ba-tung, on the old trade route to
Tibet.
Ching-hai. Kokonor, a lake in Mongolia.

97. THE NEFARIOUS WAR

戰城南

Last year we fought by the head-stream of the Sang-kan,
This year we are fighting on the Tsung-ho road.
We have washed our armor in the waves of the Chiao-
    chi lake,
We have pastured our horses on Tien-shan's snowy slopes.
The long, long war goes on ten thousand miles from home,
Our three armies are worn and grown old.

The barbarian does man-slaughter for plowing;
On his yellow sand-plains nothing has been seen but
    blanched skulls and bones.
Where the Chin emperor built the walls against the
    Tartars,
There the defenders of Han are burning beacon fires.
The beacon fires burn and never go out,
There is no end to war!—

In the battlefield men grapple each other and die;
The horses of the vanquished utter lamentable cries to
    heaven,
While ravens and kites peck at human entrails,
Carry them up in their flight, and hang them on the
    branches of dead trees.
So, men are scattered and smeared over the desert grass,
And the generals have accomplished nothing.

Oh, nefarious war! I see why arms
Were so seldom used by the benign sovereigns.

98. BEFORE THE CASK OF WINE

前有樽酒行

The spring wind comes from the east and quickly passes,
Leaving faint ripples in the wine of the golden bowl.
The flowers fall, flake after flake, myriads together.

You, pretty girl, wine-flushed,
Your rosy face is rosier still.
How long may the peach and plum trees flower
By the green-painted house?
The fleeting light deceives man,
Brings soon the stumbling age.

Rise and dance
In the westering sun,
While the urge of youthful years is yet unsubdued!
What avails to lament after one's hair has turned white
    like silken threads?

99. YUAN TAN-CHIU OF THE EAST MOUNTAIN

You, the dweller of the East Mountain,
You, the lover of the beauty of hills and valleys,
In the green spring you sleep in the empty woodland,
And hardly rise in the broad daylight.
The pine wind shakes your garment,
And the stony brook cleanses your soul.
How I envy you, who, unperturbed,
Are pillowed high in a mist of emerald!

題元丹丘山居

100. LINES

Cool is the autumn wind,
Clear the autumn moon,
The blown leaves heap up and scatter again;
A raven, cold-stricken, starts from his roost.
Where are you, beloved?—When shall I see you once
    more?
Ah, how my heart aches to-night—this hour!

101. THE BALLADS OF THE FOUR SEASONS

SPRING

The lovely Lo-foh of the land of Chin,
Is plucking mulberry leaves by the blue water.
On the green boughs her white arms gleam,
And the bright sun shines upon her scarlet dress.
"My silk-worms," says she, "are hungry, I must go.
"Tarry not with your five horses, Prince, I pray!"

Lo-foh is the heroine of a popular ballad, which was already old at Li Po's time, and which served as the basis of the present poem. The original, much longer and charmingly naïve, runs as follows:

The sun rises from the southeast nook.
It shines on the house of Master Chin.
Master Chin, he has a comely daughter.
Lo-foh is her name.

Lo-foh feeds her silk-worms well.
She picks mulberry leaves south of the city.
Her basket has a cord of blue silk;
And a hook made of a laurel branch.

Her hair is dressed in pretty knots of Wa-do;
Bright moonstones hang from her ears.
Of yellow silk is her petticoat,
And of purple silk her jacket.

[147]

The Lord Governor, he comes from the south,
His five horses stop and stay.
The Lord Governor bids his men ask;
And they say: "Who art thou, little maid?"

"I am the fair daughter of Master Chin,
"Lo-foh is my name."
"How old art thou, Lo-foh?"
"I am still less than twenty,
"But more than fifteen—yea, much more."

The Lord Governor, he entreats Lo-foh.
Says he, "Wilt thou ride with me, yea or nay?"
Lo-foh comes forward and replies:
"My Lord Governor," says she, "how foolish, indeed!
"My Lord Governor, you have your own lady,
"And Lo-foh, she has a man of her own."

102. THE BALLADS OF THE FOUR SEASONS

SUMMER

On the Mirror Lake three hundred *li* around
Gaily the lotus lilies bloom.
She gathers them—Queen Hsi-shih, in Maytime!
A multitude jostles on the bank, watching.
Her boat turns back without waiting the moonrise,
And glides away to the house of the amorous Yueh king.

Queen Hsi-shih.   See Note under No. 43.

103. THE BALLADS OF THE FOUR SEASONS

AUTUMN

The moon is above the city of Chang-an,
From ten thousand houses comes the sound of cloth-
    pounding;
The sad autumn wind blows, and there is no end
To my thought of you beyond the Jewel Gate Pass.
When will the barbarian foe be vanquished,
And you, my beloved, return from the far battlefield?

Cloth-pounding is the ironing part in the old-fashioned Chinese lauudering process. On account of the hardness of the wooden stand and mallet employed for it, the pounding produces a shrill metallic sound. Women working late, and their mallets clanging through the night, have long been a popular theme for poets.

In the present poem the situation is pathetic since from the ten thousand houses, where women are working late in the night, men have gone to the far battle front.

The Jewel Gate Pass, is located at the western extremity of Kansu province.

104. THE BALLADS OF THE FOUR
SEASONS

WINTER

The courier will depart on the morrow for the front.
All night she sews a soldier's jacket.
Her fingers, plying the needle, are numb with cold;
Scarce can she hold the icy scissors.
At last the work is done; she sends it a long, long way,
Oh, how many days before it reaches him in Lin-tao?

---

*Lin-tao, a town on the frontier of Tu-fan, whose war-
like tribes had harassed the Chinese empire for centuries
past.*

[151]

105. TWO LETTERS FROM CHANG-KAN—I

(A river-merchant's wife writes)

I would play, plucking flowers by the gate;
My hair scarcely covered my forehead, then.
You would come, riding on your bamboo horse,
And loiter about the bench with green plums for toys.
So we both dwelt in Chang-kan town,
We were two children, suspecting nothing.

At fourteen I became your wife,
And so bashful that I could never bare my face,
But hung my head, and turned to the dark wall;
You would call me a thousand times,
But I could not look back even once.

At fifteen I was able to compose my eyebrows,
And beg you to love me till we were dust and ashes.
You always kept the faith of Wei-sheng,
Who waited under the bridge, unafraid of death,
I never knew I was to climb the Hill of Wang-fu
And watch for you these many days.

I was sixteen when you went on a long journey,
Traveling beyond the Keu-Tang Gorge,
Where the giant rocks heap up the swift river,
And the rapids are not passable in May.
Did you hear the monkeys wailing
Up on the skyey height of the crags?

Do you know your foot-marks by our gate are old,
And each and every one is filled up with green moss?

The mosses are too deep for me to sweep away;
And already in the autumn wind the leaves are falling.
The yellow butterflies of October
Flutter in pairs over the grass of the west garden.
My heart aches at seeing them. . . .
I sit sorrowing alone, and alas!
The vermilion of my face is fading.

Some day when you return down the river,
If you will write me a letter beforehand,
I will come to meet you—the way is not long—
I will come as far as the Long Wind Beach instantly.

Chang-kan is a suburb of Nanking.

The Long Wind Beach, or Chang-feng Sha, is in An-hwei, several hundred miles up the river, from Nanking. It is really a long way. But by making the wife say that the way is not long, Li Po brings out the girlishness of the speaker.

Wang-fu means "husband watching" and more than one hill has taken that name because of a similar tradition of a forlorn wife who climbed the height to watch for the return of her husband.

Wei Sheng. 6th century B. C. He was a young man of fidelity. He promised to meet a girl under a bridge in Chang-an, and waited for her there. Though the girl did not appear and the river water was rising, he would not leave his post and was drowned.

106. TWO LETTERS FROM CHANG-KAN—II

(Another river-merchant's wife writes)

I lived in my maiden bower,
Unaware of all things of the world.
Since married to you of Chang-kan town,
I wander the river bank to spy the weather.
In May the south wind blows,
I think of you sailing down to Pa-ling;
In August the west wind arises,
And I know you will part from Yangtzu.
You come and go, I sorrow ever,
Seeing you so little, and living so much apart.
When will you arrive at Hsiang-tan?
My dream goes over the wind-tossed waves.
Last night a storm went past in fury,
Tearing down trees on the riverside,
Spreading darkness without end—
Where were you, then, poor traveler?
Would I could ride the swift-drifting cloud,
And meet you in good time east of Orchid Beach!

Oh, the happy pair of mandarin-ducks among the
    reed,
And the purple kingfishers, embroidered on the gold
    screen!
Why at fifteen years and little more,
My face pink like the peach flower,

Have I become a river merchant's wife,
To grieve over winds and grieve again over waves!

Pa-ling, is another name for Yo-chow, Hunan.
Hsiang-tan, in Chang-sha fu, Hunan.
[155]

107. ON ASCENDING THE SIN-PING TOWER

An exile, I ascend this tower,
Thinking of home, and with the anguish of the waning
    year.
The sun has set far beyond heaven's immensity;
The unsullied waters flow on in bleak undulation.
I see a stray cloud of Chin above the mountain trees,
And the wild geese of Tartary flying over the river dunes.
Alas! for ten thousand miles under the dark blue sky
As far as my eyes can reach, there is but one vast gloom
    for me.

---

*Both the stray cloud and the migratory birds remind
the poet of his own wanderings.*

108. ON GOING TO VISIT A TAOIST RECLUSE ON MOUNT TAI-TIEN, BUT FAILING TO MEET HIM

A dog barks afar where the waters croon.
The peach flowers are deeper-tinted, wet with rain.
The wood is so thick that one espies a deer at times,
But cannot hear the noon bell in this lonely glen.
The wild bamboos sway in the blue mist,
And on the green mountainside flying cascades glisten
What way has he gone? There is none to tell;
Sadly I lean against a pine tree here and there.

Mount Tai-tien is where Li Po used to live, and is known also as the Tai-kuang Mountain. Tu Fu mention it in one of his poems addressed to Li Po. See No. 127. "So to your old place of reading in Mount Kuang."

[157]

109. AT THE CELL OF AN ABSENT MOUNTAIN PRIEST

尋
山
僧
不
遇
作

By a stony wall I enter the Red Valley.
The pine-tree gate is choked up with green moss;
There are bird-marks on the deserted steps,
But none to open the door of the priest's cell.
I peer through the window and see his white brush
Hung on the wall and covered with dust.
Disappointed, I sigh in vain;
I would go, but loiter wistfully about.
Sweet scented clouds are wafted along the mountainside,
And a rain of flowers falls from the sky.
Here I may taste the bliss of solitude
And listen to the plaint of blue monkeys.
Ah, what tranquility reigns over this ground!
What isolation from all things of the world!

The white brush is carried by the priest as a symbol of purity and cleanliness.

110. ON A MOONLIGHT NIGHT

望
月
有
懷

The stream reflects the lean foliage of a pine—
An old pine of unremembered years.
The cold moonlight gleams on the tremulous water,
And pours into my room by the window door.
I prolong my futile singing to-night,
Deploring thee—how deeply, O prince!
For no more shalt thou see a true vassal like An-tao.
My song, ceasing, leaves the grief in my heart.

This is a poem composed probably after the rebellion of An Lu-shan and the flight of the emperor from the capital, the "prince" referring to the emperor.

111. A VISIT TO YUAN TAN-CHIU IN THE MOUNTAINS

Forth to sylvan retreats I went, a vagabond,
Led by pleasure, and of the distance unaware.
The blue range yonder lay too far to travel
When the giddy sun was ready to set.
Barely had I crossed three, four hills;
The road had taken a thousand and ten thousand turns.

I heard the monkeys wail in the still twilight,
And saw the clouds roll away one by one.
Now came the dainty moon over the tall pines,
How exquisite the autumnal scene of a hollow glen!
There was old snow left in the deep ravine,
And the frosty rapids flew, cutting through rock.

Mountains thrust their peaks in the mid-sky;
I could have climbed and gazed forever
When Tan-chiu, my friend, called me from afar.
He looked at me and burst into laughter.

I went to his hermitage down the valley
And entered the solitude of a recluse.
Here we delighted ourselves night-long—
It was lucid day-break when I spoke of going.

112.   A MIDNIGHT FAREWELL

By a pale lantern—under the cold moon
We were drinking heavily together.
Frightened by our orgies, a white heron
Flaffed out of the river shallows.   It was midnight.

送殷淑

113.   THE SONG OF LUH SHAN

侍御虛舟　廬山謠寄盧

Really I am a mad man of Chu,
Singing the phoenix-bird song and laughing at the sage
　　　Confucius.
At dawn a green jade staff in my hand,
I leave the Yellow Crane House and go,
Seeking genii among the Five Mountains, forgetting the
　　　distance.
All my life I've loved to visit the mountains of renown.

The Luh Shan looms near the constellation of the South
　　　Dipper,
Like a nine-fold screen adorned with embroidery of
　　　clouds;
And the clear lake reflects its gleaming emerald.
The two peaks shoot up high where the Gold Gate opens
　　　wide;
And over against the far waterfall of the Censer Moun-
　　　tain
The cascades of San-shi-liang hang like the Silver River
　　　of heaven.
The craggy ranges over-reach the azure blue;
And girdled in pink mist and green foliage,
They glisten in the morning sun.
The birds cannot fly over—to the remote skies of Wu.
I ascend the high place and look out on heaven and
　　　earth.
Lo! the waters of the great Kiang flow on and on never
　　　to return.

Anon, blowing yellow clouds miles upon miles, the wind
    arises,
And through the nine provinces white billows roll on
    like mountains of snow.

I love to make the song of Luh Shan.
Luh Shan is my joy and inspiration.
I gaze idly into the Stone Mirror to cleanse my soul,
Though the path Prince Shieh went is lost under deep
    green moss.
I've swallowed early the sacred pellet and forsaken all
    worldly desires.
Playing on the harp thrice over, I've attained the Way.
I see genii amid the iridescent clouds afar,
Going up to the celestial city with lotus in their hands.
I shall meet the Illimitable above the ninth heaven,
Then, with Lu-ao I hope to journey to the Great Void.

Luh Shan is a mountain near Kiu-kiang, Kiangsi.

*When Confucius was visiting the land of Chu, a mad
man named Tsu Yu passed him by, laughing and singing, "O phoenix bird, O phoenix bird!" etc. The sage
attempted in vain to have an interview with him.*

*The last stanza refers to the poet's Taoistic attainment
and visions.*

114.　TO HIS WIFE ON HIS DEPARTURE—I

別
内
赴
徵

Thrice my prince has called.　I shall go, and not return.
To-morrow morn I take leave of you,
And cross the pass of Wu Kuan.
In vain you shall look for me in the white jade house,
But you must go and climb the Hill of Wang-fu long-
　　ingly.

*These three poems were written in 755 when he was
setting out to join Li Ling, the prince of Yung.*

*As to the significance of the Hill of Wang-fu, see the
note under No. 105.　There was a hill by that name near
Hsuan-cheng, Anhwei.*

115. TO HIS WIFE ON HIS DEPARTURE—II

別内赴徵二

At the gate you still hold me by the robe,
And ask me when I shall come back from the west.
I will return some day, wearing, perhaps, a seal of gold.
And you will not imitate the wife of Su Chin,
Who came not down from her loom.

Su Chin (died B. C. 317) was a native of Lo-yang. In his youthful years he went out, seeking for a career, but returned in rags and tatters. His wife would not take the trouble of leaving her place at the loom in order to greet him. However, he succeeded later in his scheme of the federation of six weaker states against the strong state of Chin, and he was appointed prime minister of each of the six states thus combined. A seal of gold was given to a state minister as the symbol of authority.

In this poem Li Po's political ambition is evident.

[165]

別
内
赴
徵
三

116. TO HIS WIFE ON HIS DEPARTURE—III

Gold are the staircases, and like a kingfisher's wings
Sparkle the towers of the house where I shall be.
But the thought of you, my dear, who will stand alone
By the ancient gate and weep,
Will make me sit awake at night by the lonely lamp,
And watch the dying moon of dawn;
And all my tears shall flow as I journey on to the west.

117. ON HIS WHITE HAIR

On the face of the bright mirror, I wonder,
Whence has come this hoar frost of autumn!
Ah, my long, long white hair of three thousand *chang*,
Grown so long with the cares of this world!

---

*Chang is a Chinese unit of measure equal, perhaps, to
ten feet. White hair 30,000 feet is certainly long. But
this is not ludicrous to Chinese taste, for it is not a foolish
extravagance but an innocent form of poetic indulgence.*

*In Chinese literature figures such as one thousand,
three thousands, and ten thousands, simply denote a large
number. So we read constantly of a party of ten thousand guests, a waterfall three thousand feet high, and a
man emptying one thousand jugfuls of wine.*

[167]

118. TO THE HONORABLE JUSTICE HSIN

流
夜
郎
贈
辛
判
官

Once we dwelt in the city of Chang-an
In wild ecstasy of flowers and willow-green.
We drank our wine from the same bowls
With five princes and seven dukes.
Our hearts rose and grew blither,
Unflinching in the presence of a warrior lord;
Nor did we fall behind any one, when,
Delighting in wind and stream, we sought beauty.

You had red cheeks, then; and I was young, too.
We sped our horses to Chang-tai's pleasure mart,
And lightly carried our crops of gold;
Offered our essays in the court examination;
And sat feasting at a tortoise table;
And there was endless singing and dancing; . . .
We thought it would last forever, you and I—
How were we to know that the grass would tremble
And the wind and dust come, roaring down?

Down through the Han-ku Pass
The Tartar horsemen came.
I am an exile now, traveling heavy-hearted,
Far away to the land of Yeh-lang.
The peach and plum trees by the palace
Are opening their petals toward the light—
Ah, when will the Gold Cock bring me pardon,
And I may return to you from banishment?

The Gold Cock was displayed as symbol for amnesty.

[168]

119. ON HEARING THE FLUTE IN THE YELLOW CRANE HOUSE

A wandering exile, I came away to Long Beach.
I gazed toward home, beyond the horizon,
Toward the city of Chang-an.
I heard some one in the Yellow Crane House,
Playing on the sweet bamboo flute
The tune of the "Falling Plum Flowers" . . .
It was May in the waterside city.

與史郎中欽聽黃
鶴樓上吹笛

120. ON HEARING THE FLUTE AT LO-CHENG ONE SPRING NIGHT

Whence comes this voice of the sweet bamboo,
Flying in the dark?
It flies with the spring wind,
Hovering over the city of Lo.
How memories of home come back to-night!
Hark! the plaintive tune of "Willow-breaking." . . .

The "Willow-breaking" was a popular parting song.

121. ON THE TUNG-TING LAKE—I

Westward from Tung-ting the Chu River branches out,
While the lake fades into the cloudless sky of the south.
The sun gone down, the autumn twilight steals afar over
    Chang-sha.
I wonder where sleep the lost queens of Hsiang of old.

---

*These are two of the five poems Li Po composed at a
boat party with Chia-chi and Li Hua while on his way
to Yeh-lang. See the Introduction.*

*The Chu River. The Yangtze takes this name in this
vicinity near the Tung-ting Lake, which comprises the ancient land of Chu.*

*The lost queens of Hsiang, i. e. O Huang and Hu Yin,
the wives of Shun, who perished near the lake by the
Hsiang River. See No. 92.*

陪族叔刑部侍郎曄及
中書賈舍人至遊洞庭二

122. ON THE TUNG-TING LAKE—II

The autumn night is vaporless on the lake.
The swelling tide could bear us on to the sky.
Come, let us take the moonlight for our guide,
And sail to buy our drink where the white clouds are!

123.   TO HIS WIFE

Divided from you, I lament alone under the skies of
    Yeh-lang.
In my moonlit house seldom a message arrives;
I watch the wild geese all go north in the spring.
And they come south—but not a letter from Yu-chang

南流夜郎寄内

*This is evidently addressed to his last wife, who was
staying at Yu-chang, in central Kiangsi, while Li Po was
traveling westward to his place of banishment.*

[173]

124. TO HIS FRIEND, WEI, THE GOOD GOVERNOR OF CHIANG-HSIA WRITTEN IN COMMEMORATION OF THE OLD FRIENDSHIP DURING THE DAYS OF HIS BANISHMENT AFTER THE TUMULT OF WAR

Once I sought the City of White Jade in heaven,
The five palaces and twelve lofty towers,
Where gods of felicity stroked me on the forehead,
And I bound my hair and received the everlasting life.
Woe to me, I turned to the pleasures of the world,
Pondering deep on peace and war,
And the reigns of the ninety-six illustrious kings,
Whose empty fame hangs on the drifting vapor!
I could not forget the tumultuous battles;
Fain would I try the empire-builder's art
Of staking heaven and earth in one throw,
And win me the car and cap of the mandarin.
But time ordained a dire disappointment,
I threw my hopes and went, wandering wide.
I learned swordsmanship and laughed at myself.
I wielded my pen—what did I achieve after all?
A sword could not fight a thousand foemen;
The pen did steal fame from the four seas—
Yet it is a child's play not worth talking about,
Five times I sighed; and went out of the western metropolis.

At the time of my leaving
My hat-strings were wet with tears.
It was you, my friend, excellent and wise,

[174]

The peerless flower of our race,
Who spread the mat and drew the curtains round
For a parting feast to comfort me journeying far.
You came to see me off, you and your company on horse-
    back,
As far as the Inn of Cavaliers.
There amid songs and tinkling bells,
Ere our hearts were sated,
The garish sun fell beyond the Kun-ming Lake.[1]

In October I arrived in the land of Yu Chow,[2]
And saw the legions of star-beaming spears.
The northland by the sea, abandoned by our dear emperor,
And trusted to one like the monstrous whale,
That drinks up a hundred rivers at one draught,
Was crumbling fast to utter ruin.
Knowing this, I could not speak out,
And vainly wished I had lived in the fabled isle without
    care.
I was like an archer who, cowed by the wolf,
Sets the arrow but dares not draw the bow-string.
At the Gold Pagoda I brushed my tears
And cried to heaven, lamenting King Chao.
There was none to prize the bones of a swift steed.
In vain the fleet Black Ears bounced lustily,
And futile it was, should another Yo-I appear.

I plodded on, a houseless exile—
All things went amiss;
I sped my horse and returned to your town.
I met you and listened to your song and twanging strings,
Sitting ceremoniously in your flower-painted room.
Your prefecture alone possessed the peace of antiquity

And the balmy ease that lulled the mystical king Hsi to
    sleep.
You called for musicians, and the hall was gay:
Our banquet table laden with wine cups and jars,
And handsome files of men sitting with moth-eyebrowed
    girls,
Our feast went on in the light of blazing cressets.
Drunken, we danced amid the confusion of silken stools,
And round the rafters hovered our clear song—
So our revelry lasted till even after the dawn.
But you returned to Hsing-yang, your official days over.[3]
What a multitude that gathered for the farewell rites,
And those tents erected on the roadside near and far!
Once parted, we were divided by a thousand miles,
With our fortunes differing like summer and winter.

Summers and winters had come and gone—how many
    times?—
And suddenly the empire was wrecked.
The imperial army met the barbarian foe,
The dust of the battlefield darkened sky and sea,
And the sun and moon were no longer bright
While the wind of death shook the grass and trees.
And the white bones were piled up in hills—
Ah, what had they done—the innocent people?

The pass of Han-ku guarded the imperial seat of splendor,
And the fate of the empire hung on General Ku Shu.
He with his thirty thousand long-spear men
Surrendered, and opened the gate to the savage horde.
They tamed the courtiers like dogs and sheep,
And butchered the men who were loyal and true.

To His Friend, Wei, the Good Governor

Both the sovereign and the heir fled from the palace,
And the twin imperial cities were laid to waste.
The imperial prince, given the supreme command,[4]
Held his armies in the stronghold of Chu;
But there was no discipline of Huan and Wen.
His generals herded bears and tigers in the ranks,
And men wavered in doubts and fears
While the rebellion raged like tempest.
You were defending Fang-ling, I remember,
With loyalty unsurpassed in all ages.

I lived then in the mountain of Incense Burner,
Eating the mist and washing my mouth in the crystal
    fountain.
The house door opened on the winding Nine Rivers,
And beneath my pillow lay the five lakes, one linked to
    another.
When the fleet came upstream in the midnight
And filled the city of Hsin-yang with flags and banners,
I, betrayed by my own empty name,
Was carried by force aboard the war-boat.
They gave me five hundred pieces of gold,
I brushed it away like a rack, and heeded not;
Spurned the gift and the proffered title—
For all that I was banished to the land of Yeh-lang.

Oh, the long road of a thousand miles to Yeh-lang!
The westward journey made me old.
Though the world was being put to order,
I was ignored like a stalk of frost-bitten grass.
The sun and the moon shine alike on all—
How could I complain of injustice to heaven?

[177]

You, good governor, adored like a god,
Took compassion on your old friend.
You invited me to be your guest of honor,
And we ascended three times the tower house of Yellow
     Crane.
I blushed to think of Mi Hsien, the poet-recluse—
How he would sit, looking complacently at the Parrot Isle.
No more heroes were born to the enchanted mountains of
     Fan.[5]
And the desolation of autumn covered the world.
But lo, the river swelling with the tides of Three Canyons,
And the thousands of junks that thronged these waters,
Jostling their white sails, gliding past to Yang-chow!
On looking out on these things, my grief melted away
     in my heart.

We sat by the gauze-curtained window that opened to the
     sky
And over the green trees that grew like hair by the
     waterside,
Watching the sun with fear lest it be swallowed by the
     mountains,
And merry at moonrise, drinking still more wine.

Those maids of Wu and pretty girls of Yueh,
How dainty their vermilioned faces!
They came up by the long flight of stairs; emerged,
From behind the bamboo screen, smiling;
And danced, silken-robed, in the wind of spring.

The host was reluctant to pause
Though the guests knelt and asked for rest.
You showed me your poem of Ching-shan,

Rivaling the native beauty of the lotus,
That rises from the lucent water, unadorned.
Your joyous spirit swelling over in your heart,
You called for me ever at your residence,
Your mansion whose red gate was guarded by men,
Holding their spears in stately rows.
Amid quaintly cut stones and trimmed bamboos
A rivulet ran, brimming with limpid water.
We went up and sat in the waterside pavilion,
And poured forth our souls in heroic discourses.
A word between us is precious like white jade,
And a pledge of ours more than yellow gold.
I was not unworthy of you, I venture to say,
And swore by the Blue Bird on my fidelity.

The happy magpie among the five-colored clouds
Came, flying and crying, from heaven.
The mandate of my pardon arrived, I was told,
And I could return from banishment in Yeh-lang.
It was as if warmth enlivened the frozen vale,
Or fire and flame sprang from the dead ashes.

Still the dogs of Chieh bark at Yao,[5]
And the Tartar crew mock at the imperial command.
In the middle of the night I sigh four and five times,
Worrying ever over the great empire's affairs.
Still the war banners cover the sides of the two mountains,
Between which flows the Yellow River.
Our generals like frightened fowls dare not advance,
But linger on, watering their idle horses.
Ah, where shall we find a Hu-I, the archer,
Who with the first arrow will shoot down the evil star?

¹ *This, the longest poem in the entire collection of Li Po's works, is in a way his autobiography. It was written after he was allowed to return from banishment in 759. See the* Introduction.

The first stanza tells of his early life of seclusion in the world of Taoistic visions; of his ambition; and of his disappointment at Chang-an, the western metropolis.

The Inn of Cavaliers and the Kun-ming Lake are both situated in the vicinity of Chang-an. At the time of Li Po's departure from the capital (circa 745) Wei was evidently in Chang-an and was able to give him the big farewell demonstration described herein.

² *Yu Chow, the northland, is in the present Chili province. It was here that An Lu-shan was stationed with his star-gleaming legions, and Li Po detected the Tartar general's rebellious schemes, though he was obliged to keep silent. It was this region which comprised the state of Yen in the 4th century B. C. and where King Chao ruled and built the Gold Pagoda.*

King Chao once questioned his retainer, Kuo Wei, as to the ways of attracting the great men of the time to his court. Kuo Wei told his liege the following parable:

Once upon a time a certain king sent out his servant on a mission to secure a swift horse that could run a thousand li in a day. The servant returned with a bagful of bones of a horse which was said to have made a thousand li in a day. For these remains the servant had paid 500 pieces of gold. The king was angry, for he wanted a live horse. The servant replied, "When the world learns that your Majesty has spent 500 pieces of gold on a dead horse, the live ones will arrive without your looking for

them." Indeed, three horses—all of them, one thousand
li runners—arrived soon at the court.

"So my king," continued Kuo Wei, "if you really desire to show your high regard for men of great talent,
begin with me who have but small talent!"

King Chao took the advice. He built the Gold Pagoda,
and there he waited upon Kuo Wei as his teacher. Then
many men of ability came from all parts of China to King
Chao, and with their aid he became the most powerful of
all kings.

The Black Ears was a famous swift horse.

Yo-I was one of those great men who came to King
Chao. Li Po laments that now there is no sovereign
seeking as earnestly as King Chao for men of talent. And
these, of whom he is one, have no opportunity.

[3] Just in what prefecture Wei was stationed is not
known. When his official term was over, he returned to
Hsin-yang, a town on the west side of Chang-an. Sometimes the two names are applied synonymously to the
capital.

The Chinese made a great deal of leave-taking, often
erecting as in this case tents on the wayside and offering
sacrifices to the god of the road for the safety of the one
setting out on his journey.

These passages refer, of course, to the rebellion of An
Lu-shan. General Ku Shu defended the Han-ku Pass,
which is an older name for Tung Kuan. By the twin imperial cities the poet very probably means Hsing-yang
and Chang-an, unless he means the latter and the city of
Lo-yang. See the Introduction.

[4] The imperial prince i. e. Li Ling, the Prince of Yung.
See the Introduction.

Li Po was quite willing to join the staff of the prince at the beginning; but when his rebellious intent became obvious, the poet retired to the mountain of Luh, near Kiu-kiang, or Hsin-yang, as it was called at the time. The Incense Burner is one of the peaks of the Luh mountain range.

Wei was now the governor of Chiang-hsia, a district in southern Ḥupeh. The Yellow Crane House (See note, No. 40) looks over the Yangtze-kiang.

⁵ Chieh is a notorious tyrant, and Yao a benign sovereign, of ancient China. By the "dogs of Chieh" are meant Shih Ssu-ming and his cohorts, who kept up the rebellion started by An Lu-shan.

Hu I, a famous archer of the legend, who shot down the false suns that appeared in the heavens and devastated the crops. Here Li Po means a savior, who could deliver the empire from the clutch of the rebels.

PART II

POEMS BY OTHER POETS
CONCERNING LI PO

PART II

The following poems by Tu Fu and others are but a few of many such collected by Wang Chi and appended to his edition of Li Po's Complete Works. These poems are not only beautiful in themselves but are of a peculiar interest in that they give a glimpse into the charming circle of poets by whom Li Po was surrounded and esteemed so highly.

125. THE EIGHT IMMORTALS OF
THE WINECUP

飲
中
八
仙
歌　杜
甫

CHI-CHANG rides his horse, but reels
    As ِ n a reeling ship.
Should he, blear-eyed, tumble into a well,
    He would lie in the bottom fast asleep.
JU-YANG PRINCE must have three jugfuls.
    Ere he goes up to court.
How copiously his royal mouth waters
    As a brewer's cart passes by!
It's a pity, he mournfully admits,
    That he is not the lord of the Wine Spring.
Our MINISTER LI squanders at the rate
    Of ten thousand pence per day.
He inhales like a great whale,
    Gulping one hundred rivers;
And with a cup in his hand insists,
    He loves the *sage* and avoids the *wise*.
TSUNG-CHI, a handsome youth fastidious,
    Disdains the rabble,
And turns his gaze toward the blue heaven,
    Holding his beloved bowl—
Radiant is he like a tree of jade
    That stands against the breeze.
SU CHIN, the religious, cleanses his soul
    Before his painted Buddha,
But his long rites must needs be interrupted
    As oft he loves to go on a spree.

As for LI PO, give him a jugful,
   He will write one hundred poems.
He drowses in a wine shop
   On a city-street of Chang-an;
And though his sovereign calls
   Will not board the imperial barge.
"Please your Majesty," says he,
   "I am a god of wine."
CHANG HSU is a caligrapher of renown,
   Three cups makes him the master.
He throws off his cap, baring his pate
   Unceremoniously before princes,
And wields his inspired brush—lo!
   Wreaths of cloud roll on the paper.
CHAO SUI, another immortal, elate
   After full five jugfuls,
Is eloquent with heroic speech,
   The wonder of all the feasting hall.

TU FU.

---

*The Wine Spring, located in the western part of Kansu,
is said to have possessed a natural fountain of wine.
The sage and the wise. See No. 126.*

126. THE EX-MINISTER

Avoiding the *wise*, I've resigned
    From the empire's ministry.
Loving the *sage*, still I sip
    The soothing cup of wine.

Ah, those eager visitors of yesterday,
    Who flocked at the front of my gate—
How many of them have come
    This morning, I pray?

                 —LI SHIH-CHI

天寶五載初罷相作李適之

A book called "Facts about Poets" says: "In the latter part of the Kai-yuan Era (A. D. 713-742) the prime minister, Li Shih-chi, had an enviable reputation for his simplicity and rugged uprightness. Li Ling-fu hated him, and by slander and intrigue caused his retirement. All those at the court knew the innocence of Shih-chi, but the emperor neglected to consult him. Fretting under this mistreatment, Shih-chi drank wine daily and also made poems." Of which this is a specimen. He describes the solitude and ease of his private life.

By "avoiding the wise" is meant vacating one's official position in order to make way for the wise and talented. The phrase, first used by Shih Ching of the Han dynasty in his petition for his release from the office of the premier, had become a stock pretext for the retiring official.

[187]

On the other hand, the thick wine was called the wise, *and the clear wine the* sage. *Hence, there is in this poem a play on words with a subtle irony, of a kind much relished by the literary Chinese.*

127.   A VISIT TO FAN WITH LI PO

My honored friend, Li, writes excellent verses,
That ring at times like Ying-kao's masterly lines.
I, too, a sojourner of Tung Meng,
Love him as a younger brother loves the elder.
Drunk, we sleep both under one cover at night;
And in daytime we go together hand in hand.
Now longing for a place of quiet company,
We come to visit you on the city's northside.
Your little boy waits on us so handsomely,
Joy leaps in our hearts as we enter your gate.
What solitude!   We hear only the chilly mallets,
And see the clouds bivouac before the old city wall.
Having always sung the ode of the sweet citron,
Who cares to seek for the soup of the water-herbs?
You desire not the debasement of official life,
But remain untrammeled like the blue, boundless sea.

Tu Fu.

與李十二同尋范十隱居杜甫

This poem was written in the earlier days of their friendship when Li Po and Tu Fu were both in Shantung.   Tung Meng is a district in that province.

128. PARTING WITH LI PO ON THE TUNG-TING LAKE

To-day at the time of falling leaves we meet only to part
On the autumn waters of the Tung-ting, that stretch afar
    to the horizon.
And while talking together of our good old time at the
    metropolis of gold,
We turn to the northern sky and gaze at the stars of the
    Ursa Major, our eyes filled with tears.

CHIA CHI.

---

*The metropolis of gold is the capital of the empire,
Chang-an, where both Li Po and Chia Chi had spent
their more prosperous days.*

129. AN INVITATION TO LI PO

In the cool autumn month—the Eight or the Ninth—
White is the dew, and desolate the garden arbor.

As I sat weary, devoid of the heart's buoyancy,
I heard the wind whisper to the leaves on the tree-top,
And longed to see some friend, a man of learning and
valor,
With whom I could discourse over the past and the pres-
ent,
When suddenly who should come but you, Honorable Li.

I greeted you with joy, regretting only it had not been
sooner.
I clapped my hands at your enchanting utterances;
We talked metaphysics; we bubbled with laughter.
You expounded the vicissitudes of the past dynasties,
And made visible the exploits of kings and conquerors.

A knap-sack on your back, filled with books,
You go a thousand miles and more, a pilgrim.
Under your sleeve there is a dagger,
And in your pocket a collection of poems.
Your eyes shine like luminous orbs of heaven
When you recite your incomparable songs and odes.
You sip wine and twang your lute strings
When the winter's breath congeals the crystaline frost.

To-day I laid bare before you
All things long stored in my heart.

[191]

Now my family has a villa,
Situated on the north side of Mount Sung.
One sees the bright moon rise over the peak,
And the chaste beams silver the transparent stream.
The clouds scatter, and the house is quiet;
The passing wind bears the aroma of pine and cassia.
If you will deign to make a visit thither with me,
I will not forget the honor for a thousand years.

TSUI TSUNG-CHI.

Tsui Tsung-chi, the handsome man and the fourth of the Immortals in Tu Fu's poem. He was a good friend of Li Po, and there are a number of poems extant, that were written by the latter to him. See the Introduction.

Mount Sung, one of the five sacred mountains, is to the southeast of Honan-fu, Honan.

130.   TO LI PO ON A SPRING DAY

Po, the poet unrivaled,
In fancy's realm you soar alone.
Yours is the delicacy of Yui,
And Pao's rare virility.
Now on the north of the Wei River
I see the trees under the vernal sky
While you wander beneath the sunset clouds
Far down in Chiang-tung.
When shall we by a cask of wine once more
Argue minutely on versification?

Tu Fu.

春日憶李白杜甫

---

*Yui and Pao refer respectively to Yui Hsin and Pao
Chao, both noted poets of the 6th century.*

131. TO LI PO

Long have I not seen you, Li.
Poor man, for your feigned madness
The world would have you die.
But my heart dotes on your gifted soul
For the thousand poems of your nimble wit,
For the one wine-cup—your penury's balm.
So to your old place of reading in Mount Kuang
Come back, O white-headed one! It is time.

                                        TU FU.

---

*Written possibly after the incarceration of Li Po at
Kiu-kiang and while the death sentence was hanging over
his white head.*

132.   THE GRAVE OF LI PO

By the River of Tsai-shih
There is Li Po's mound
Amid the endless plains of grass
That stretch to the cloud-patched sky.
Alas! here under the fallow field
The bones of him lie whose writing once
Startled heavens and shook the earth.
Of all poets, unfortunate as they be,
There is none wretcheder, Master, than you.

Po Chu-i.

李白之墓

白居易

*It is likely that Po Chu-I visited the grave of Li Po
during his banishment at Kiu-kiang, 815-818.*

[195]

BIOGRAPHICAL NOTES
ON LI PO
BY CHINESE AUTHORS

PART III

The following translations are offered as much because of their contents as because of the interest they possess as types of ancient Chinese writing at and about Li Po's time.

Li Yang-ping's Preface is written in the euphuism of the Six Dynasty Period with its parallel constructions, profuse classical allusions, and curious hyperboles. Though the author's judgment is not worth any serious consideration, this is the first critical essay on Li Po.

The two biographies from the "Books of Tang," in spite of their brevity and mistakes, remain still the official and only extant authentic accounts of the poet's life written in Chinese.

THE PREFACE TO THE FIRST EDITION OF THE POETIC WORKS OF LI TAI-PO
by
LI YANG-PING[1]
MAGISTRATE OF TANG-TU, HSUAN-CHOU, OF THE TANG DYNASTY

Li Po, surnamed Tai-po, was a man of Cheng-chi of Lunghsi and a descendant in the ninth generation from Kao, who was the king Wu-chao of the Liang state.

His early ancestors, one after another, wearing the gem and girdle,[2] were possessed of pre-eminence and renown. Later one Li, though he had done no wrong, was exiled and dwelt in the land of Chiao-chi, where he changed his names. The five generations from Chiung-shan to the emperor Shun were in the peasantry; and so were the Li's, and they did not shine greatly. Which is a thing to be lamented.

In the beginning of the Shen-lung era[3] the family escaped and returned to Shuh. Our "Po-yang"[4] was born,

---

[1] Li Yang-ping, Li Po's kinsman, and a calligrapher of note, brought out the poet's works in 762.

[2] "Wearing gem and girdle" implies holding governmental office.

[3] The Shen-lung era covers the years 705 and 706. The statement here is obviously a mistake since by this time Li Po was already a boy of four or five. The New Book of Tang incorporates this mistake.

[4] Po Yang. The surname of Laotzu, the founder of Taoism, who was born in 604 B. C. miraculously from the left side of the mother. And at his birth he pointed to a plum tree. Here Li Yang-ping alludes to Li Po metaphorically.

pointing to the plum tree. On the evening of his birth his mother dreamed of the planet of Chang-keng. So when the babe was born, he was named Po, and surnamed Tai-po. They said he was begotten by the spirit of the Great White Star.

He would read nought but the books of the sages and was ashamed to write after the lewd school of Chen and Wei.[5] Thus, his words resembled the speech of the heavenly genii. His writing consists of many satires and allegories.

From the ages of the Three Dynasties[6] and the times of the *Feng* and *Sao*,[7] there has been but one man, our master, who could run the race with Chu and Sung, and who could whip and spur Yang and Ma.[8] Yea, our master walks alone in the history of a thousand years. Is it any wonder that he swayed princes and earls who hurried to him, arraying their multitudinous arms and linking the cross-bars of their carriages while numerous men of wisdom gathered to do homage as the birds flock to the Phoenix?

The Lord of the Yellow Gate[9] says that it is the

---

[5] Chen and Wei are the names of states under the Chou dynasty, which contributed love songs to the Book of "Odes" compiled by Confucius.

[6] The Three Dynasties. The Hsia, the Shang and the Chou, comprising the years 2205-255 B. C.

[7] Feng and Sao are styles of ancient poetry. The Feng is found in the Confucian "Odes" while the Sao originated with Chu and Sung (i. e. Chu Yuan and Sung Yu) of the 4th and 3rd centuries B. C.

[8] Yang and Ma. Yang Hsiung (53 B. C.—A. D. 18) and Ssuma Hsiang-ju (died 117 B. C.), two noted poets of the Han Dynasty.

[9] The Lord of Yellow Gate. Refers to a certain Lu, a successful statesman as well as a gentleman of parts.

Censor of the Court, Chen,[10] who stayed the tide of decadence and wrought a change of literature in form and matter. But even under our present dynasty the poesy was infected with the manners of the seraglio school of the Liang and Cheng dynasties[11] until our master swept them and banished them from the earth, causing a marvelous change. Now the books of poesy, new or old, are cast off and do not prevail. But the writings of our master cover the universe. He in his power may be said to rival Nature, the creator and transformer.

In the beginning of the Tien-pao era[12] his Majesty's grandsire deigned to summon him. At the Gate of Gold Horse the emperor alighted from his car and walked to meet our master, welcoming him as though he were the venerable Chi the Hoary;[13] granted him a feast on the table of seven jewels and made him eat, seasoning the soup for him with his august hands. He said: "Thou art a cotton-clothed one, but art become known to me. How could this have been but that thou hast cherished virtue and righteousness?" So the Emperor let him sit in the Hall of Gold Bells, and go in and out of the Han-ling Academy; and questioned him on the affairs of government and privily ordered him to compose mandates and rescripts. Of this none was aware.

---

10 Censor of the Court, Chen. Chen Tsu-ang, a poet and an intimate friend of Lu above.

11 The Liang and Chen dynasties covered respectively A. D. 502-556 and 557-587, preceding the Tang dynasty.

12 The Tien-Pao era covers the years 742-755.

13 Chi, the Hoary. Refers to Chi Li-chi, one of the so-called "Four Gray-heads," of the 3rd century B. C., who withdrew from the world toward the close of the reign of the First Emperor of the Chin dynasty, but who reappeared upon the establishment of the Han dynasty and were welcomed and venerated by the new emperor.

But when the true and the base are put side by side, the gifted one is injured and slanders are made, while the candid word of virtue fails. The emperor neglected him. Our master drank wine and by his indulgence obscured himself. And when he made poems and songs, he spoke often of the East Mountain. With Ho Chi-chang, Tsui Tsung-chi and the rest, he did also the revel of the Eight Immortals. Chi-chang called him "a god in exile." So his comrades at the court made compositions, entitled "The Song of the God in Exile," which were several hundred in number, and most of which mentioned our master's disappointments in life. The Son of Heaven, knowing that he could not be retained, gave gold and let him depart.

Thereafter he went with Yen-yun, visiting-inspector of Chen-liu,[14] to the High Heavenly Priest of Pe-hai, whom he petitioned and was bestowed the Taoist tablet at the Purple Peak Temple in Chi-chou.[15] He only desired to return east to Peng-lai[16] and ride with the *winged man* to the Scarlet Hill of immortality.

I, Yang-ping, was then trying my harp-playing and singing[17] at Tang-tu, although it was not what my heart coveted. Our master, forsaking me not, took a skiff and came to see me. It was when I was about to hang

[14] Chen-liu. A city near Kaifeng-fu, Honan.

[15] Chi-chou. The present city, Chinan-fu, Shantung.

[16] Peng-lai is a fabled island in the eastern sea; and the Scarlet Hill a dwelling place of exalted spirits. The Winged Men are those who have attained the highest rank in the Taoist Orders.

[17] To do "harp-playing and singing" means simply to govern, the phrase having a classic allusion to the story of the legendary emperor Shun of whom it is written, "Shun sang the Song of the South Wind, and there was peace in the land." Here the writer simply means that he, Yang-ping, was governor of Tang-tu.

up my mandarin cap[18] that our master sickened. His manuscripts in ten thousand bundles and his hand collections were not yet arranged. So while lying on his pillow, he delivered them to me to be put in order. In discoursing on the significations of the *Kuan-chu,* now I feel ashamed to Pu Shang;[19] while in expounding the words of the *Spring and Autumn* I must forever blush before Tu Yu.

Since confusion befell the mid imperial plains,[20] our master sought refuge elsewhere for eight years. His writings of those years were lost, nine out of ten. What are preserved herein, are for the most part what I obtained from others.

Done on the I-chiu, the 11th moon of the First Year of the Pao-ying Era. (762.)

---

18 To "hang up one's mandarin cap" is to resign from office. Yang-ping was transferred from Tang-tu to Chin-yun Chekiang, in 763.

19 Pu-shang (born, 507 B. C.), a disciple of Confucius, had the distinction of being entrusted by his master with the famous collection of Odes, the "Shi King," of which Kuan-chu forms a part. Tu Yu of the 3rd century, A. D., was a celebrated commentator on another Confucian classic, the *Spring and Autumn.* By his metaphorical allusions to these eminent men and books Li Yang-ping means to exalt the works of Li Po which he is editing and commenting upon.

20 The "Confusion," of the "mid imperial plains" refers to the Rebellion of An Lu-shan which was started in 755.

LI PO—A BIOGRAPHY by LIU HSU

(From the "Old Book of Tang"[1])

Li Po, surnamed Tai-po, was a man of Shantung.[2] While young, he possessed a superior talent, a great and tameless spirit, and fantastical ways of a transcendent mind. His father was Captain of Jen-cheng, and there Po made his home. While young still, he with the youths of Luh—Kung Chao-fu, Han Chun, Pei-Cheng, Chang Shu-ming, and Tao-Mien—retired in the mountain of Chu-lai, where they drank wine freely amid blithe singing. They were known at the time as "the Six Idlers of the Bamboo Valley."

Early in the Tien-pao era Po went traveling to Kuei-chi. He retired to a district in Yen with a Taoist, whose name was Wu-yun. Yun was called and went up to the imperial palace. He recommended Po to the court. And they were both ordered to wait upon the emperor in the Han-ling Academy.

Po loved wine as hithertofore; and with his drinking companions drowsed daily in the tavern.

The emperor Hsuan Tsung arranged tunes and desired to have new words for the court music. At once he

---

[1] Li Hsu (897-947) wrote the "Old Book of Tang," a chronicle of the Tang dynasty, with a large number of biographies. The book was completed in 934.

[2] Li Po was not born in Shantung, but made his home there for a time as is told in the Introduction. Jen-cheng is a city in Shantung.

summoned Po from the Tavern where he lay. Men took water and dashed it on his face, after which he was made to hold the writing brush. Anon, he composed ten or more songs. The emperor was much pleased withal.

Once while dead drunk in the palace hall Po held out his feet and made Kao Li-shih to pull off his shoes. Because of this he was dismissed and sent away.

Now he wandered over lakes and rivers. He drank heavily all day long. At this time Tsui Tsung-chi, the Court Historian, demoted, was serving at Chin-ling. With Po he matched poems and drank wine. One moonlight night they took a boat from Tsai-shih to Chin-ling. Arrayed in the palace robe of brocade, Po sat in the boat, laughed and rolled his intrepid eyes as though there were no mortals near him. Ere this, Ho Chi-chang met Po and praised him, saying, "This man is a god exiled from the heaven above."

In the rebellion of Luh-shan the emperor Hsuan Tsung made his progress to the land of Shuh. On his way he appointed Ling, Prince of Yung, as supreme Military Commander of Chiang and Hwai Regions and Governor-general of Yang-chou. Po was at Hsuan-Chou, and had an audience of the prince, and at last entered his service. Prince of Yung plotted conspiracy, and was defeated in the war. Po, involved, was sentenced to perpetual banishment to Yeh-lang. Later he was pardoned and enabled to return. He died at last at Hsuan-cheng with too much drinking. There are twenty volumes of his writing which prevail at this time.

LI PO—A BIOGRAPHY by SUNG CHI

(From the "New Book of Tang"[1])

Li Po, surnamed Tai-po, is a descendant in the ninth generatioñ from the emperor Hsing-sheng. His ancestor in the latter part of the Sui dynasty was for some wrong-doing exiled to the west barbarian land; but the family escaped and returned in the beginning of the Shen-lung era. They sojourned in Pa-hsi.

At the time of Po's birth his mother dreamed of the planet of Chang-keng, and because of this he was named after the star. At ten years of age he was versed in "the Odes" and "the History." When he was grown up, he hid himself in the Min Mountain, and would not respond though the province called for men of talent.

Su Ting became Governor of I-chou. On seeing Po, he wondered and said: "This lad is a genius, he is brilliant and singular. If a little more learning be added, he may be compared with Hsiang-ju." But Po delighted in strategems of crisscross alliances, took to swordsmanship, and to errantry, scorning riches but esteeming alms-giving.

Later he sojourned in Jen-cheng; and with Kung Chao-fu, Han Chun, Pei Cheng, Chang Shu-ming, and Tao-mien, dwelt in the Chu-lai Mountain, daily drinking

---

[1] The "New Book of Tang" was finished in 1060 by Ou-yang Hsiu and Sung Chi. Sung Chi, who did all the biographies in this book died in 1061.

till they sank to the ground. They called themselves, "the Six Idlers of the Bamboo Valley."

At the beginning of the Tien-pao era he journeyed south to Kuei-chi, where he made a friend of Wu-Yun. Yun was summoned to court. So arrived Po also at Chang-an. He went to see Ho Chi-chang. Chi-chang saw his writing and said with a sigh, "You are a god in exile." He spoke to the emperor Hsan Tsung. Po was given audience in the Hall of Golden Bells; he discoursed upon the affairs of the world, and presented an ode. The emperor made him eat, seasoning the soup for him. A rescript was issued, by which Po was appointed to serve in the Han-ling Academy.

Po still went with his drinking companions, and drowsed in the market place.

The emperor sat in the Pavilion of Aloes. Stirred by a fancy, he desired to obtain Po to write songs to music. Po was summoned in, and he was drunk. The attendants took water and washed his face. When he recovered somewhat, he was handed a writing brush, and made compositions. Exquisite and graceful and finely finished they were, yet he made them without stopping to think. The emperor liked Po's talent, and often banqueted with him.

Once while attending upon the emperor, Po grew drunk and made Kao Li-shih pull off his shoes for him. Li-shih, a favorite of the throne, was humiliated thereby. He pointed out to Yang Kuei-fei a poem of Po, and caused her wrath. So when the emperor desired to appoint Po to office, then she stopped him.

Po himself, knowing he could not be taken in by those near the throne, all the more abandoned himself to recklessness. With Ho Chi-chang, Li Shih-chi, Chin,

Prince of Ju-nan, Tsui Tsung-chi, Su Chin, Chang-Hsu, and Chiao Sui, he made up the "Eight Immortals of the Wine-cup." He implored for permission to return to the mountains; and the emperor gave gold and let him go.

Po roamed hither and thither. One time he took a boat with Tsui Tsung-chi from Tsai-shih to Chin-ling. Arrayed in the palace robe of brocade, he sat in the boat as though there were no mortal near him.

At the time of An Lu-shan's rebellion Po lingered between the Su-sung and the Kuang-luh mountains. Ling, Prince of Yung, called him and made him a subordinate of his staff. When Ling started war, Po fled to Peng-tse. But with the fall of Ling, Po was sentenced to death. Ere this, when Po was stopping in Ping-chou, he met Kuo Tsu-i and admired him. Once Tsu-i broke the law, and Po came to rescue and had him freed. So now Tsu-i petitioned to ransom Po with his own rank and title whereupon a rescript was issued for his perpetual banishment at Yeh-lang.

He received pardon, and returned to Hsin-yang. There he was imprisoned on account of a certain affair,[2] when Sung Jo-ssu on his way to Honan with his army of three thousand men of Wu came to Hsin-yang, released the prisoner, and placed Po on his general staff. But before long he resigned. When Li Yang-ping became Governor of Tang-tu, Po went to live with him.

Emperor Tai Tsung ascended the throne,[3] and he sum-

---

[2] This story of Li Po's second incarceration and his subsequent relations with Sung Jo-ssu is not authentic. Sung Jo-ssu was the man who memorialized the throne on behalf of Li Po at the occasion of the latter's imprisonment.

[3] Tai Tsung ascended the throne in 763.

moned Po to take the office of the censor of the court; but Po was then dead. His years were sixty and a little more.

In his old age Po was fond of Taoism. He crossed the Bull Rock Shoal and reached Ku-shu,[4] where the Green Hill of the House of Hsieh pleased him, and he wished to make it the place of his last rest. But when he died, he was buried at the East Base.

In the beginning of the Yuan-ho era[5] Fan Chuan-cheng, Inspector of Hsuan-she, performed rites at his grave, and forbade woodcutting at the place. He sought for descendants of his. There were only two grand-daughters, who were married and were wives of peasants, but who carried with them an air of refinement. They wept and said, "Our grandfather wanted the Green Hill; but is buried at the East Base, that is not his true wish." Whereupon Chuan-cheng made a reburial and erected two monuments. He told the two women that he would marry them into the official class. They declined, saying, "It is our destiny to end in poverty and isolation. We desire not to re-marry." Chuan-cheng approved them, and relieved their husbands from the conscript labor for the state.

In the reign of the emperor Wen Tsung[6] by imperial edict Po in songs and odes, Pei-min in sword dance, and Chang Hsu in cursive calligraphy, were declared "the Three Paragons."

---

[4] Ku-shu, is not far from Tang-tu, which is an old name for Taiping, Anhwei.

[5] Yuan-ho era. 806-820.

[6] Wen Tsung reigned during 827-841.

BIBLIOGRAPHY

NOTES ON THE CHINESE TEXTS

Very shorty after the death of Li Po, Li Yang-ping published a collection in ten books with a preface dated 762, in which he says that the poet had lost a large portion of the poems written during his wanderings after the Rebellion of An Lu-shan, and many pieces in the books had been obtained from friends. Under the Sung Dynasty and about the year 1000, Kuo Yo-shih brought out a collection of ten books, which he combined with that of Li Yang-ping, making twenty books with 765 poems altogether, beside ten books of miscellaneous writings. In 1064 the first two of the three volumes of another collection were discovered, adding 100 new poems. Wei Hao's collection in two books was not brought to light till 1068, which contributed 44 new pieces. Thus the collection grew. In 1080 Sung Ming-chiu published the complete works in thirty books, containing nearly 1000 poems and 66 pieces in prose. Under the Ching dynasty and in 1759 Wang Chi brought out the final edition of the complete works in 30 books, with copious annotations and six books of critical, biographical and miscellaneous matter gleaned and gathered from all possible sources. This edition was reprinted in 1908 by the Soo Yeh Company of Shanghai.

Besides those enumerated above, there have been published innumerable editions of complete works and selections in past centuries. I have used a modern Japanese edition of selected poems, consulted a Chinese edition of the Sung period in the Newberry Library of Chicago, and also the original Wang Chi edition of 1759 in the New York City Public Library. The textual variations are few and unimportant as far as the poems in the present book are concerned.

TRANSLATIONS AND WORKS ON LI PO

The following books and periodicals are only the more important items of the Li Po Literature in English, French, and German, which have come to the writer's notice. The figure in parenthesis at the end indicates the number of poems of Li Po translated in the book.

Joseph Marie Amiot. *Mémoires—concernant—l'Histoire; les Sciences, Les Arts, les Moeurs, les Usages, etc. —des Chinois, par les Missionaires de Pekin.* Paris, 1776-97. 14 vols. Contains a short biographical sketch, "Ly-pe, Poête." Vol. V., Pp. 396-399.

Anna Bernhardi. *Li Tai-Po. Mitteilungen des Seminar für Orientalische Sprüche*, die Königlichen Friedrich Wilhelms Universität, Berlin, 1916. Vol. 19, Pp. 105-138. Translations with the Chinese text. Introduction, notes, list of previous translations. Also a translation of Li Yang-ping's *Preface* with the original text. (41)

Hans Bethge. "Die Chinesische Flöte." Leipzig: Inselverlag, 1910. (15)

Charles Budd. "Chinese Poems." Oxford: Oxford University Press, 1912. A discussion of Chinese versification in the Introduction. Translations in rhymed verse. (1)

L. Cranmer-Byng. "A Lute of Jade." London: J.

Murray, 1911. New York: E. P. Dutton & Co., 1918. Poems of different periods. The Introduction covers "the Poets of the Tang Dynasty" and "a Poet's Emperor" (Hsuan Tsung). (8)

—— —— "A Feast of Lanterns." London: J. Murray, 1916. New York: E. P. Dutton & Co., 1918. (6)

Joseph Edkins. "On Li Tai Po." *Journal of the Pekin Oriental Society*, 1890. Vol. II., No. 5, Pp. 317-364. A paper read before the society on December 21, 1888. Translations in rhymed verse with Chinese text. (24)

Karl Florenz. "Gedichte von Li Taipe" in "Beitrage für Chinesische Poesie." *Mitteilungen der Deutschen Geselschaft für Natur—und Völkerkunde Ostasiens,* 1889. Vol. I, Pp. 44-61. Contains a biography, notes and the original Chinese text. (12)

A. Forke. "Blüthen Chinesischer Dichtung." Magdburg, 1899. Poems of the Han, the Six Dynasties, as well as the Tang periods, done in rhymed verse. Illustrations. (39)

Judith Gautier. "Poémes Chinois de Tous les Temps." Revue de Paris, June, 1901. (3)

—— ——"Le Livre de Jade." Paris, 1867 and 1918.

—— —— "Chinese Lyrics." From "The Book of Jade" translated by James Whithall. New York: B. W. Huebsch, 1918. (9)

H. A. Giles. "Gems of Chinese Literature." London: Bernard & Quaritch, 1884. (3)

—— ——"A History of Chinese Literature." London & New York: D. Appleton & Co., 1901. Pp. 151-156. (9)

—— ——"Chinese Poetry in English Verse." London: Bernard & Quaritch, 1898. A collection of Chinese poems from different periods, some of which are scattered throughout the "History of Chinese Literature" above. (21)

Wilhelm Grübe. "Geschichte der Chinesischen Literatur." Leipzig: C. P. Amelangs Verlag, 1902. Pp. 277-284. (2)

Marquis d'Hervey Saint-Denys. "Poésie de l'Époque de Thang." Paris, 1862. An Anthology of the Tang period with notes. Biographical sketch of Li Po in the Introduction, (29)

Elizabeth Oehler-Heimerdinger. "Chinesische Lyrik," Geist Ostens, München, 1913. I Jahrgang, Heft 3, Pp. 108-118.

Théodore Pavie. "Le Poète Ly Tai-pe." "Choix des Contes et Nouvelles." Paris, 1839. The story of Li Po, one of the *nouvelles,* is entirely unreliable, though not without elements of truth. Pp. 9-142.

Ezra Pound. "Cathay." London: Elkin Mathews, 1915. (11)

Franz Toussaint. "La Flute de Jade." Paris, 1920. A collection of very free and often fragmentary translations in prose. (17)

Arthur Waley. "Li Tai-Po." *The Asiatic Review*, London, October, 1919. Vol. XV, No. 44, Pp. 584-612. A paper which was read before the China Society. A valuable introduction with a translation of the poet's Biography in the "New Book of Tang." (24)

—— —— "More Translations from the Chinese." New York: Alfred Knopf, 1919. Poems of Li Po in this book are a selection from those in the *Asiatic Review*, above.

Florence Ayscough and Amy Lowell. "Fir-Flower Tablets." Boston: Houghton, Mifflin Co., 1921. Poems translated by Mrs. Ayscough and done into English verse by Miss Lowell. Mostly from Li Po and Tu Fu. (85)

For general reference a few more books may be suggested, though they do not particularly concern Li Po.

Demetrius C. Boulger. "The History of China." London: W. Thacker & Co., 1898.

Li Ung Bing. "Outlines of Chinese History." Shanghai: the Commercial Press, 1914.

Sir John Francis Davis. "Poeseos sinicae commentari" (the Poetry of China). London: Asher & Co., 1870.

Arthur Waley. "One Hundred and Seventy Chinese Poems." New York: Alfred Knopf, 1919.

Herbert Giles. "A Chinese Biographical Dictionary." London: B. Quaritch, 1892 and 1900.

POEMS OF LI PO TRANSLATED IN THIS BOOK

Previous translations, where they exist, are noted under each poem, although the compilation is by no means exhaustive. As for the full name of the translator and the title of his book or article, see the foregoing Bibliography.

No. 1. ON THE SHIP OF SPICE-WOOD.

> Pound, *Cathay.* The River Song.
> St. Denys, *Poésie.* En Bateau.
> Toussaint, *La Flute de Jade.* Le Bonheur.
> Waley, *Asiatic Rev.* River Song.
> Lowell, *Fir-Flower Tablets.* River Chant.

No. 2. IN THE MOUNTAINS ON A SUMMER DAY.

> Waley, *Asiatic Rev. and More Translations.*
> In the Mountains on a Summer Day.

No. 3. NOCTURNE.

> Lowell, *Fir-Flower Tablets.* Autumn River Song.

No. 4. A FAREWELL SONG OF WHITE CLOUDS.

> Lowell, *Fir-Flower Tablets.* The Song of White Clouds.

No. 5. THE LONG DEPARTED LOVER.

> Bernhardi, *Li Tai-Po.* In die Ferne.

Toussaint, *La Flute de Jade.* La Chambre
Vide.

No. 6, 7, 8. LADY YANG KUEI-FEI AT THE IMPERIAL
FEAST OF THE PEONY, I, II, III.

Cranmer-Byng, *A Lute of Jade.* An Em-
peror's Love.
St. Denys, *Poésie,* Strophes Improvisées.
Toussaint, *La Flute de Jade.* Strophes Im-
provisées.
Lowell, *Fir-Flower Tablets.* Songs to the
Peonies.

No. 9. A POEM COMPOSED AT THE IMPERIAL COMMAND
IN THE SPRING GARDEN, WHILE LOOKING ON
THE NEWLY GREEN WILLOWS BY THE DRAGON
POND AND LISTENING TO THE HUNDRED-FOLD
NOTES OF THE FIRST NIGHTINGALES.

No. 10. TO HIS FRIEND DEPARTING FOR SHUH.

Edkins, *On Li Tai-Po.* Address to a Friend.
Pound, *Cathay.* Leave-taking near Shuh.

No. 11. TO HIS THREE FRIENDS.

No. 12. ADDRESSED HUMOROUSLY TO TU FU.

No. 13. ON A PICTURE SCREEN.

No. 14. ON ASCENDING THE NORTH TOWER ONE AU-
TUMN DAY.

No. 15. THE SUMMIT TEMPLE.

No. 16. LAO-LAO TING, A TAVERN.

No. 17. THE NIGHT OF SORROW.

> Edkins, *On Li Tai-Po.* Feeling Aggrieved.
> Forke, *Blüthen Chin. Dicht.* Die Weinende.
> Giles, *Gems of Chinese Lit.* Tears.
> Lowell, *Fir-Flower Tablets.* Passionate Grief.

No. 18. THE SORROW OF THE JEWEL STAIRCASE.

> Bethge, *Die Chin. Flöte.* Die Treppe im Mondlicht.
> Edkins, *On Li Tai-Po.* Grief on Marble Steps.
> Giles, *Gems of Chinese Lit.* From the Palace.
> Pound, *Cathay.* The Jewel Stair's Grievance.
> Toussaint, *La Flute de Jade.* Le Chagrin de Perron de Jade.

No. 19. THE GIRL OF PA.

> Toussaint, *La Flute de Jade.* La Femme de Pa.

No. 20, 21, 22, 23, 24. THE WOMAN OF YUEH. I, II, III, IV, V.

> Toussaint, *La Flute de Jade.* Les Jeunes Filles de Yueh. (No. 22)
> Lowell, *Fir-Flower Tablets.* The Young Girls of Yueh. (No. 21, 22)

No. 25. THE SOLITUDE OF NIGHT.

> Cranmer-Byng, *A Feast of Lanterns.* Along the Stream.

Edkins, *On Li Tai-Po.* Expressing What I
Think.

Giles, *Chinese Poetry in Eng.* The Poet.

Waley, *Asiatic Rev. and More Translations.*
Self Abandonment.

No. 26. THE MONUMENT OF TEARS.

No. 27. ON A QUIET NIGHT.

Bernhardi, *Li Tai-Po.* Gedanken in Stiller
Nacht.

Cranmer-Byng, *A Lute of Jade.* Thoughts
in a Tranquil Night.

Edkins, *On Li Tai-Po.* Thoughts on a Quiet
Night.

Florenz, *Gedichte v. Li Taipe.* Gedanken in
Stiller Nacht.

Forke, *Blüthen Chin. Dicht.* Mondenschein.

Bethge, *Die Chin. Flöte.* In der Fremde.

Giles, *Chinese Poetry in Eng.* Night
Thoughts.

———, *Hist. of Chinese Lit.* P. 154.

St. Denys. *Poésie.* Pensée dans une Nuit
Tranquille.

Toussaint, *La Flute de Jade.* Tristesse.

Lowell, *Fir-Flower Tablets.* Night Thoughts.

No. 28. THE BLUE WATER.

Bernhardi, *Li Tai-Po.* Die Weise von
Grünen Wasser.

Edkins, *On Li Tai-Po.* Song of the Green
Water.

Forke, *Blüthen Chin. Dicht.* Im Kahn.
Gautier, *Chinese Lyrics.* The Forbidden Flower.
Oehler-Heimerdinger, *Chinesche Lyric.* Im Kahn.

No. 29.   THE CHING-TING MOUNTAIN.

Edkins, *On Li Tai-Po.* Sitting Alone on a Hill.
Florenz, *Gedichte v. Li Taipe.* Einsam auf dem Berge King-ting Sitzend.
Giles, *Chinese Poetry in Eng.* Companions.
——, *Hist. of Chinese Lit.* P. 154.

No. 30.   WITH A MAN OF LEISURE.

Florenz, *Gedichte v. Li Taipe.* Zechlage mit einem Einsiedler in Gebirge.
Waley, *Asiatic Rev.* Drinking Together in the Mountains.

No. 31.   THE YO-MEI MOUNTAIN MOON.

No. 32.   ON THE CITY STREET.

No. 33.   ON THE DEATH OF THE GOOD BREWER OF HSUAN-CHENG.

Lowell, *Fir-Flower Tablets.* On the Subject of Old Tai's Wine-shop.

No. 34.   TO HIS WIFE.

Bernhardi, *Li Tai-po.* Meine Frau.

No. 35.   THE POET THINKS OF HIS OLD HOME.

Edkins, *On Li Tai-Po.* East Mountain Recollected.

No. 36, 37.   SORROW OF THE LONG GATE PALACE. I, II.

Lowell, *Fir-Flower Tablets.* Bitter Jealousy in the Palace of the High Gate.

No. 38.   AN ENCOUNTER IN THE FIELD.

Lowell, *Fir-Flower Tablets.* A Poem Given to a Beautiful Woman Encountered on a Field-path.

No. 39.   TO WANG LUN.

Lowell, *Fir-Flower Tablets.* A Parting Gift to Wang Lun.

No. 40.   ON SEEING OFF MENG HAO-JAN.

Giles, *Chinese Poetry in Eng.* Gone.
Pound, *Cathay.* Separation on the River Kiang.
Lowell, *Fir-Flower Tablets.* At the Yellow Crane Tower, Taking Leave of Meng Hao-Jan on his Departure to Kuang Ling.

No. 41.   ON BEING ASKED WHO HE IS.

No. 42.   IN THE MOUNTAIN.

Giles, *Hist. of Chinese Lit.* P. 155.
Lowell, *Fir-Flower Tablets.* Reply to an Unrefined Person Encountered in the Hills.

No. 43. THE FAIR QUEEN OF WU.

> Bethge, *Die Chin. Flöte.* Liebestrinken.
> Gautier, *Rev. d. Paris.* Ivresse d'Amour.
> ——, *Chinese Lyrics,* Intoxication of Love.
> Toussaint, *La Flute de Jade.* La Danseuse Un Peu Ivre.

No. 44. WHILE JOURNEYING.

> Giles, *Chinese Poetry in Eng.* In Exile.

No. 45. THE RUIN OF THE KU-SU PALACE.

> Toussaint, *La Flute de Jade.* Les Ruines de Sou-Tai.
> Lowell, *Fir-Flower Tablets.* A Traveler Comes to the Old Terrace.

No. 46. THE RUIN OF THE CAPITAL OF YUEH.

No. 47. THE RIVER JOURNEY FROM WHITE KING CITY.

> Edkins, *On Li Tai-Po.* From the City of White God.

No. 48, 49. BY THE GREAT WALL, I, II.

> St. Denys, *Poésie.* Chansons des Frontières. (No. 48)
> Toussaint, *La Flute de Jade.* Encore. (No. 48)
> Lowell, *Fir-Flower Tablets.* Songs of the March, III. (No. 48)

No. 50. THE IMPERIAL CONCUBINE.

> Bernhardi, *Li Tai-Po.* Acht Gedechte über die Freuden in Palastinnern.

Lowell, *Fir-Flower Tablets*. Pleasures within the Palace.

Giles, *Chinese Poetry in Eng.* A Favorite.

———, *Hist. of Chinese Lit.* P. 152.

No. 51. PARTING AT CHING-MEN.

No. 52. ON THE YO-YANG TOWER WITH HIS FRIEND CHIA.

No. 53. AWAKENING FROM SLEEP ON A SPRING DAY.

Bernhardi, *Li Tai-Po.* Der Trinke im Frühling.

Florenz, *Gedichte v. Li Taipe.* Lebensweisheit.

Forke, *Blüthen Chin. Dicht.* Im Rausch.

Giles, *Gems of Chinese Lit.* On Getting Drunk in Spring.

——— *Chinese Poetry in Eng.* The Best of Life is But—

St. Denys, *Poésie.* Un Jour de Printemps.

Toussaint, *La Flute de Jade.* Un Jour de Printemps.

Waley, *Asiatic Rev.* Waking from Drunkenness on a Spring Day.

Lowell, *Fir-Flower Tablets.* A Statement of Resolutions after Being Drunk on a Spring Day.

No. 54. THREE WITH THE MOON AND HIS SHADOW.

Bethge, *Die Chin. Flöte.* Drei Kameraden.

Florenz, *Gedichte v. Li Taipe.* Einsame Gelage im Monschein.

Giles, *Chinese Poetry in Eng.* Last Words.
——, *Hist. of Chinese Lit.* P. 153.
Grube, *Geschichte d. Chin. Lit.* Trinklieder.
Toussaint, *La Flute de Jade.* Petite Fête.
Waley, *Asiatic Rev. & More Translations.*
Drinking Alone in the Moonlight, I.
Lowell, *Fir-Flower Tablets.* Drinking Alone
in the Moonlight, I.

No. 55.   AN EXHORTATION.

Bernhardi, *Li Tai-Po.* Afforderung zum Trin-
ken.
Forke, *Blüthen Chin. Dicht.* Der Rabe.
St. Denys, *Poésie.* Chanson à Boire.
Waley, *Asiatic Rev.* Drinking Song.
Lowell, *Fir-Flower Tablets.* Drinking Song.

No. 56.   THE INTRUDER.

Bernhardi, *Li Tai-Po.* Frühlings Gedanken.

No. 57.   THE CROWS AT NIGHTFALL.

Bernhardi, *Li Tai-Po.* Des Rabens Nachtli-
cher Schrei.
Edkins, *On Li Tai-Po.* Raven Calling in the
Night.
Forke, *Blüthen Chin. Dicht.* Der Rabe.
Gautier, *Chinese Lyrics.* The Birds are Sing-
ing at Dusk.
Giles, *Hist. of Chinese Lit.* P. 155.
——, *Chinese Poetry in Eng.* For Her Hus-
band.

Cranmer-Byng, *A Lute of Jade.* Memories
with the Dusk Return.
Toussaint, *La Flute de Jade.* Les Corbeaux.

No. 58. To Meng Hao-jan.

No. 59. To Tung Tsao-chiu.

Pound, *Cathay.* Exile's Letter.
Waley, *Asiatic Rev.* Sent to the Commissary,
Yuan of Chiao City, In Memory of Former
Excursions.

No. 60. Taking Leave of a Friend.

Forke, *Blüthen Chin. Dicht.* Geleit.
Gautier, *Rev. d. Paris.* Le Depart d'un Ami.
Giles, *Chinese Poetry in Eng.* A Farewell.
Pound, *Cathay.* Taking Leave of a Friend.
Lowell, *Fir-Flower Tablets.* Saying Good-
bye to a Friend.

No. 61. Maid of Wu.

No. 62. The Lotus.

No. 63. To his Two Children.

No. 64. To a Friend Going Home.

No. 65. A Mountain Revelry.

No. 66. The Old Dust.

Giles, *Hist. of Chinese Lit.* P. 155.

No. 67. A PAIR OF SWALLOWS.

Toussaint, *La Flute de Jade*. La Fidélité.

No. 68. AT A RIVER TOWN.

No. 69. I AM A PEACH TREE.

No. 70. THE SILK SPINNER.

No. 71. CHUANG CHOU AND THE BUTTERFLY.

No. 72. THE POET MOURNS HIS JAPANESE FRIEND.

Edkins, *On Li Tai-Po*. A Japanese Lost at Sea.

No. 73. IN THE SPRING-TIME ON THE SOUTH SIDE OF THE YANGTZE-KIANG.

No. 74. THE STEEP ROAD TO SHUH.

Waley, *Asiatic Rev*. The Ssuchuan Road.
Lowell, *Fir-Flower Tablets*. The Perils of the Shu Road.

No. 75. PARTING AT A TAVERN OF CHIN-LING.

Waley, *Asiatic Rev*. Parting with Friends at a Wine-shop in Chin-ling.
Lowell, *Fir-Flower Tablets*. The Poet is Detained in a Nanking Wine-shop on the Eve of Starting on a Journey.

No. 76. THE PHOENIX BIRD TOWER.

Bernhardi, *Li Tai-Po*. Aufstieg auf dem Turme des Phoeniz-Paares in Chin-ling.

Pound, *Cathay.* The City of Cho-An.
Lowell, *Fir-Flower Tablets.* Feng Huang Tai.

No. 77. HIS DREAM OF THE SKY-LAND: A FAREWELL
POEM.

Waley, *Asiatic Rev.* A Dream of Tien-Mu
Mountain (a partial translation).

No. 78. IN MEMORIAM.

No. 79. ON THE ROAD OF AMBITION.

No. 80. TO TU FU FROM SAND HILL CITY.

Lowell, *Fir-Flower Tablets.* A Poem Sent to
Tu Fu from Sha Chiu Cheng.

No. 81. A VINDICATION.

Waley, *Asiatic Rev. and More Translations.*
Drinking Alone in the Moonlight, III.
Lowell, *Fir-Flower Tablets.* Drinking Alone
in the Moonlight, II.

No. 82. TO LUH, THE REGISTRAR.

No. 83. TO THE FISHERMAN.

No. 84. THE TEARS OF BANISHMENT.

No. 85. THE LOTUS GATHERER.

Bethge, *Die Chin. Flöte.* Am Ufer.
Cranmer-Byng, *A Lute of Jade.* On the
Banks of Jo-yeh.
Gautier, *Chinese Lyrics.* At the River's Edge.

St. Denys, *Poésie.* Sur les Bords de Jo-Yeh.
Toussaint, *La Flute de Jade.* Sur les Bords
de Jo-Yeh.
Waley, *Asiatic Rev.* On the Banks of Jo-Yeh.

No. 86. THE SPORT FELLOWS.

Forke, *Blüthen Chin. Dicht.* Die Kameraden.

No. 87. THE DANCING GIRL.

No. 88. THE ROVER OF CHAO.

Forke, *Blüthen Chin. Dicht.* Der Fahrende
Ritter.
Grube, *Geschichte d. Chin. Lit.* Ballade vom
Fahrenden Ritter. P. 282.
St. Denys, Poésie. Le Brave.
Toussaint, *La Flute de Jade.* La Gloire.

No. 89. TO HIS FRIEND IN CHIANG-HSIA.

No. 90, 91. THE CATARACT OF LUH SHAN, I, II.

Florenz, *Gedichte v. Li Taipe.* Der Wasser-
fall am Lushan. (No. 90)

No. 92. BEREFT OF LOVE.

Waley, *Asiatic Rev.* The Distant Parting.

No. 93, 94. LADY WANG CHAO-KUN, I, II.

Lowell, *Fir-Flower Tablets.* The Honorable
Lady Chao. (No. 94)

No. 95. THE NORTH WIND.

No. 96. THE BORDERLAND MOON.

> Bernhardi, *Li Tai-Po.* Der Mond über dem Kuan Berge.
> Lowell, *Fir-Flower Tablets.* The Moon over the Mountain Pass.

No. 97. THE NEFARIOUS WAR.

> Forke, *Blüthen Chin. Dicht.* Elend des Krieges.
> Waley, *Asiatic Rev.* Fighting.
> Lowell, *Fir-Flower Tablets.* Fighting to the South of the City.

No. 98. BEFORE THE CASK OF WINE.

> Bernhardi, *Li Tai-Po.* Zwei Lieder beim Becher Wein.
> Forke, *Blüthen Chin. Dicht.* Beim Wein.

No. 99. YUAN TAN-CHIU OF THE EAST MOUNTAIN.

> Bernhardi, *Li Tai-Po.* Schreiben an Yuan Tan-Chiu.
> Waley, *Asiatic Rev.* To Tan-chiu.

No. 100. LINES.

> Bernhardi, *Li Tai-Po.* Gedichte aus Zeilen von Drei, Fünf und Sieben Zeichen.
> Giles, *Chinese Poetry in Eng.* No Inspiration.
> Lowell, *Fir-Flower Tablets.* Word Pattern.

No. 101, 102, 103, 104. THE BALLADS OF THE FOUR SEASONS.

Bernhardi, *Li Tai-Po.* Vier Wu Lieder nach Tsu-yeh Art.

St. Denys, *Poésie.* Chanson des Quatre Saisons.

Toussaint, *La Flute de Jade.* Chanson des Quatre Saisons.

Cranmer-Byng, *A Lute of Jade.* Under the Moon. (No. 103)

Giles, *Gems of Chinese Lit.* The Grass-Widow's Song. (No. 103)

No. 105, 106. Two Letters from Chang-Kan.

Bernhardi, *Li Tai-Po.* Zwei Lieder aus Chang-Kan.

Florenz, *Gedichte v. Li Taipe.* Das Lied von Chang-Kan. (No. 105)

Pound, *Cathay.* The River Merchant's Wife: A Letter. (No. 105)

Waley, *Asiatic Rev.* Chang-Kan. (No. 105)

Lowell, *Fir-Flower Tablets.* Chang-Kan. (No. 105)

No. 107. On Ascending the Sin-ping Tower.

Florenz, *Gedichte v. Li Taipe.* Beim Aufsteigen im Hause, Sin-Ping-Lou.

No. 108. On Visiting a Taoist Recluse on Mount Tai-Tien, but Failing to Meet Him.

Florenz, *Gedichte v. Li Taipe.* Vergeblicher Besuch bei einem Einsiedler.

Lowell, *Fir-Flower Tablets.* Visiting Taoist

Priest on the Mountain that which Upholds Heaven; He is Absent.

No. 109. At the Cell of an Absent Mountain Priest.

Florenz, *Gedichte v. Li Taipe.* Besuch bei einem Bergpriester, den Ich Nicht Antraf.

No. 110. On a Moonlight Night.

Florenz, *Gedichte v. Li Taipe.* Gedanken beim Betrachten des Mondes.
Lowell, *Fir-Flower Tablets.* In Deep Thought, Gazing at the Moon.

No. 111. A Visit to Yuan Tan-chiu in the Mountains.

No. 112. A Midnight Farewell.

No. 113. The Song of Luh Shan.

Edkins, *On Li Tai-Po.* Song of Lushan.
Florenz, *Gedichte v. Li Taipe.* Lied auf dem Lushan.

No. 114, 115, 116. To his Wife on his Departure.

Lowell, *Fir-Flower Tablets.* Separated by Imperial Summons from Her who Lives Within.

No. 117. On his White Hair.

Giles, *Hist. of Chinese Lit.* P. 153.
——, *Chinese Poetry in Eng.* Within a Mirror.

Oehler-Heimerdinger, *Chinesische Lyric.* Wenn All mein Weisses Haar.

No. 118. TO THE HONORABLE JUSTICE HSIN.

No. 119. ON HEARING THE FLUTE IN THE YELLOW CRANE HOUSE.

No. 120. ON HEARING THE FLUTE IN LO-CHENG ONE SPRING NIGHT.

Lowell, *Fir-Flower Tablets.* Hearing a Bamboo Flute on a Spring Night in the City of Lo Yang.

No. 121, 122. ON THE TUNG-TING LAKE, I, II.

No. 123. TO HIS WIFE.

No. 124. TO HIS FRIEND WEI, THE GOOD GOVERNOR OF CHIANG-HSIA. WRITTEN IN COMMEMORATION OF THE OLD FRIENDSHIP DURING THE DAYS OF HIS BANISHMENT AFTER THE TUMULT OF WAR.

No attempt was made to list previous translations for the following poems in Part II.

No. 125. THE EIGHT IMMORTALS OF THE WINE-CUP.
TU FU.

No. 126. THE EX-MINISTER OF STATE. LI SHIH-CHI.

No. 127. A Visit to Fan with Li Po.   Tu Fu.

No. 128. Parting with Li Po on the Tung-Ting Lake.   Chia Chi.

No. 129. An Invitation to Li Po.   Tsui Tsung-chi.

No. 130. To Li Po on a Spring Day.   Tu Fu.

No. 131. To Li Po.   Tu Fu.

No. 132. The Grave of Li Po.   Po Chu-i.

THE END

Chinese Poet

he

Date Due

李 太 白 詩 （原文）

一、江上吟

木蘭之枻沙棠舟。玉簫金管坐兩頭。美酒樽中置千斛。載妓隨波任去留。仙人有待乘黃鶴。海客無心隨白鷗。屈平詞賦懸日月。楚王臺榭空山丘。興酣落筆搖五嶽。詩成笑傲凌滄洲。功名富貴若長在。漢水亦應西北流。

二、夏日山中

懶搖白羽扇。躶體青林中。脫巾挂石壁。露頂灑松風。

三、秋浦歌

淥水淨素月。月明白鷺飛。郎聽採菱女。一道夜歌歸。

四、白雲歌。送劉十六歸山。

楚山秦山皆白雲。白雲處處長隨君。長隨君。君入楚山裏。雲亦隨君渡湘水。湘水上。女蘿衣。白雲堪臥君早歸。

五、寄遠

美人在時花滿堂。美人去後餘空牀。牀中繡被卷不寢。至今三載聞餘香。香亦竟不滅。人亦竟不來。相思黃葉落。白露濕青苔。

六、清平調一

雲想衣裳花想容。春風拂檻露華濃。若非群玉山頭見。會向瑤臺月下逢。

七、清平詞二

一枝穠艷露凝香。雲雨巫山枉斷腸。借問漢宮誰得似。可憐飛燕倚新粧。

八、清平調三

名花傾國兩相歡。長得君王帶笑看。解釋春風無限恨。沈香亭北倚闌干。

[1]

九、侍從宜春苑。奉詔賦龍池
柳色初青。聽新鶯百囀歌。

東風已綠瀛洲草。紫殿紅樓覺春好。池南柳色半青
青。縈煙裊娜拂綺城。垂絲百尺挂雕楹。上有好鳥
相和鳴。間關早得春風情。春風卷入碧雲去。千門
萬戶皆春聲。是時君王在鎬京。五雲垂暉耀紫清。
仗出金宮隨日轉。天回玉輦繞花行。始向蓬萊看舞
鶴。還過茝石聽新鶯。新鶯飛繞上林苑。願入簫韶
雜鳳笙。

一〇、送友人入蜀

見說蠶叢路。崎嶇不易行。山從人面起。雲傍馬頭
生。芳樹籠秦棧。春流遶蜀城。升沈應已定。不必
問君平。

一一、送韓準、裴政、孔巢父、還山。

獵客張兔罝。不能掛龍虎。所以青雲人。高歌在巖
戶。韓生信英彥。裴子含清真。孔侯復秀出。俱與雲
霞親。峻節凌遠松。同衾臥盤石。斧冰嗽寒泉。三子

同二展。時時或乘興。往往雲無心。出山揖牧伯。長
嘯輕衣簪。昨宵夢裏還。云弄竹溪月。今辰魯東門。
帳飲與君別。雪崖滑去馬。蘿徑迷歸人。相思若烟
草。歷亂無冬春。

一二、戲贈杜甫

飯顆山頭逢杜甫。頂戴笠子日卓午。借問別來太瘦
生。總為從前作詩苦。

一三、觀元丹丘坐巫山屏風

昔遊三峽見巫山。見畫巫山宛相似。疑是天邊十二
峰。飛入君家綵屏裏。寒松蕭颯如有聲。陽臺微茫
如有情。錦衾瑤席何寂寂。楚王神女徒盈盈。高咫
尺。如千里。翠屏丹崖粲如綺。蒼蒼遠樹圍荊門。歷
歷行舟泛巴水。水石潺湲萬壑分。煙光草色俱氤
氳。溪花笑日何年發。江客聽猿幾歲開。使人對此
心緬邈。疑入嵩丘夢綵雲。

一四、秋登宣城謝朓北樓

江城如畫裏。山晚望晴空。兩水夾明鏡。雙橋落彩

虹。人煙寒橘柚。秋色老梧桐。誰念北樓上。臨風懷謝公。

一五、題峰頂寺

夜宿峰頂寺。舉手捫星辰。不敢高聲語。恐驚天上人。

一六、勞勞亭

天下傷心處。勞勞送客亭。春風知別苦。不遣柳條青。

一七、怨情

美人捲珠簾。深坐蹙蛾眉。但見淚痕濕。不知心恨誰。

一八、玉階怨

玉階生白露。夜久侵羅襪。卻下水晶簾。玲瓏望秋月。

一九、巴女詞

巴水急如箭。巴船去若飛。十日三千里。郎行幾歲歸。

二〇、越女詞 一

長干吳兒女。眉目艷星月。屐上足如霜。不著鴉頭襪。

二一、越女詞 二

吳兒多白皙。好爲蕩舟劇。賣眼擲春心。折花調行客。

二二、越女詞 三

耶溪採蓮女。見客棹歌回。笑入荷花去。佯羞不出來。

二三、越女詞 四

東陽素足女。會稽素舸郎。相看月未墮。白地斷肝腸。

二四、越女詞 五

鏡湖水如月。耶溪女如雪。新粧蕩新波。光景兩奇絕。

二五、自　　遣

對酒不覺暝。落花盈我衣。醉起步溪月。鳥還人亦
稀。

二六、襄　陽　曲

峴山臨漢江。水綠沙如雪。上有墮淚碑。青苔久磨
滅。

二七、靜　夜　思

牀前看月光。疑是地上霜。舉頭望山月。低頭思故
鄉。

二八、綠　水　曲

綠水明秋月。南湖採白蘋。荷花嬌欲語。愁殺蕩舟
人。

二九、獨　坐　敬　亭　山

眾鳥高飛盡。孤雲獨去閒。相看兩不厭。只有敬亭
山。

三○、山　中　與　幽　人　對　酌

兩人對酌山花開。一杯一杯復一杯。我醉欲眠卿且
去。明朝有意抱琴來。

三一、峨　眉　山　月　之　歌

峨眉山月半輪秋。影入平羌江水流。夜發清溪向三
峽。思君不見下渝州。

三二、相　逢　行

相逢紅塵內。高揖黃金鞭。萬戶垂楊裏。君家阿那
邊。

三三、哭　宣　城　善　釀　紀　叟

紀叟黃泉裏。還應釀老春。夜臺無李白。沽酒與何
人。

三四、贈　　內

三百六十日。日日醉如泥。雖爲太白婦。何異太常
妻。

三五、憶　東　山

不向東山久。薔薇幾度花。白雲還自散。明月落誰家。

三六、長　門　怨　一

天廻北斗挂西樓。金屋無人螢火流。月光欲到長門殿。別作深宮一段愁。

三七、長　門　怨　二

桂殿長愁不記春。黃金四屋起秋塵。夜懸明鏡青天上。獨照長門宮裏人。

三八、陌上贈美人

駿馬驕行踏落花。垂鞭直拂五雲車。美人一笑褰珠箔。遙指紅樓是妾家。

三九、贈　汪　倫

李白乘舟將欲行。忽聞岸上踏歌聲。桃花潭水深千尺。不及汪倫送我情。

四○、黃鶴樓送孟浩然之廣陵

故人西辭黃鶴樓。煙花三月下揚州。孤帆遠影碧空盡。唯見長江天際流。

四一、答湖州迦葉司馬問白是何人

青蓮居士謫仙人。酒肆藏名三十春。湖州司馬何須問金粟如來是後身。

四二、山　中　問　答

問余何意棲碧山。笑而不答心自閑。桃花流水杳然去。別有天地非人間。

四三、口號吳王美人半醉

風動荷花水殿香。姑蘇臺上見吳王。西施醉舞嬌無力。笑倚東窗白玉床。

四四、客　中　行

蘭陵美酒鬱金香。玉椀盛來琥珀光。但使主人能醉客。不知何處是他鄉

[5]

四五、蘇臺覽古

舊苑荒臺楊柳新。菱歌淸唱不勝春。只今惟有西江
月。曾照吳王宮裏人。

四六、越中覽古

越王勾踐破吳歸。義士還家盡錦衣。宮女如花滿春
殿。只今惟有鷓鴣飛。

四七、早發白帝城

朝辭白帝彩雲間。千里江陵一日還。兩岸猿聲啼不
住。輕舟已過萬重山

四八、塞 下 曲 一

塞虜乘秋下。天兵出漢家。將軍分虎竹。戰士臥龍
沙。邊月隨弓影。胡霜拂劍花。玉關殊未入。少婦莫
長嗟。

四九、塞 下 曲 二

白馬黃金塞。雲砂遶夢思。那堪愁苦節。遠憶邊城

兒。螢飛秋窻滿。月度霜閨遲。摧殘梧桐葉。蕭颯沙
棠枝。無時獨不見。流淚空自知。

五〇、宮 中 行 樂 詞

小小生金屋。盈盈在紫微。山花挿寶髻。石竹繡羅
衣。每出深宮裏。常隨步輦歸。只愁歌舞散。化作綵
雲飛。

五一、渡 荊 門 送 別

渡遠荊門外。來從楚國遊。山隨平野盡。江入大荒
流。月下飛天鏡。雲生結海樓。仍連故鄉水。萬里送
行舟。

五二、與夏十二登岳陽樓

樓觀岳陽盡。川廻洞庭開。雁引愁心去。山衘好月
來。雲間連下榻。天上接行杯。醉後凉風起。吹入舞
袖廻。

五三、春 日 醉 起 言 志

處世若大夢。胡爲勞其生。所以終日醉。頽然臥前

橙。覺來盼庭前。一鳥花間鳴（借間此何時。春風語
流鶯，感之欲歎息。對酒還自傾。浩歌待明月。曲盡
已忘情。

五四、月下獨酌

花間一壺酒。獨酌無相親。舉杯邀明月。對影成三
人。月既不解飲。影徒隨我身。暫伴月將影。行樂須
及春。我歌月徘徊。我舞影零亂。醒時同交歡。醉後
各分散。永結無情遊。相期邈雲漢。

五五、將 進 酒

君不見黃河之水天上來。奔流到海不復廻。君不見
高堂明鏡悲白髮。朝如青絲暮成雪。人生得意須盡
歡。莫使金樽空對月。天生我材必有用。千金散盡
還復來。烹羊宰牛且爲樂。會須一飲三百杯。岑夫
子。丹丘生。進酒君莫停。與君歌一曲。請君爲我側
耳聽。鐘鼓饌玉不足貴。但願長醉不願醒。古來聖
賢皆寂寞。惟有飲者留其名。陳王昔時宴平樂。斗
酒十千恣讙謔。主人何爲言少錢。徑須沽取對君

酌。五花馬。千金裘。呼兒將出換美酒。與爾同銷萬
古愁。

五六、春 思

燕草如碧絲。秦桑低綠枝。當君懷歸日。是妾斷腸
時。春風不相識。何事入羅幃。

五七、烏 夜 啼

黃雲城邊烏欲棲。歸飛啞啞枝上啼。機中織錦秦川
女。碧紗如煙隔窗語。停梭悵然憶遠人。獨宿空房
淚如雨。

五八、贈孟浩然

吾愛孟夫子。風流天下聞。紅顏棄軒冕。白首臥松
雲。醉月頻中聖。迷花不事君。高山安可仰。徒此把

五九、憶舊遊寄譙郡元參軍

憶昔洛陽董糟丘。爲余天津橋南造酒樓。黃金白璧
買歌笑。一醉累月輕王侯。海內賢豪青雲客。就中

與君心莫違。廻山轉海不作難。傾情倒意無所惜。
我向淮南攀桂枝。君留洛北愁夢思。遊相
隨。相隨迢迢訪仙城。三十六曲水迴縈。一溪初入
千花明。萬壑度盡松風聲。銀鞍金絡倒平地。漢東
太守來相迎。紫陽之眞人。邀我吹玉笙。餐霞樓上
動仙樂。嘈然宛似鸞鳳鳴。袖長管催欲輕舉。漢中
太守醉起舞。手持錦袍覆我身。我醉橫眠枕其股。
當筵意氣凌九霄。星離雨散不終朝。分飛楚關山水
遙。余既還山尋故集。君亦歸家渡渭橋。君家嚴君
勇貌虎。作尹幷州遏戎虜。五月相呼度太行。摧輪
不道羊腸苦。行來北涼歲月深。感君貴義輕黃金。
瓊杯綺食青玉案。使我醉飽無歸心。時時出向城西
曲。晉祠流水如碧玉。浮舟弄水簫鼓鳴。微波龍鱗
莎草綠。興來攜妓恣經過。其若楊花似雪何。紅粧
欲醉宜斜日。百尺清潭寫翠娥。翠娥嬋娟初月輝。
美人更唱舞羅衣。清風吹歌入空去。歌曲自繞行雲
飛。此時行樂難再遇。西遊因獻長楊賦。北闕青雲
不可期。東山白首還歸去。渭橋南頭一遇君。鄲臺

之北又離群。問余別恨知多少。落花春暮爭紛紛。
言亦不可盡。情亦不可極。呼兒長跪緘此辭。寄君
千里遠相憶。

六〇、送 友 人

青山橫北郭。白水遶東城。此地一爲別。孤蓬萬里
征。浮雲游子意。落日故人情。揮手自茲去。蕭蕭班
馬鳴。

六一、對 酒

蒲萄酒。金叵羅。吳姬十五細馬馱。青黛畫眉紅錦
靴。道字不正嬌唱歌。玳瑁筵中懷裏醉。芙蓉帳裏
奈君何。

六二、古 風

碧荷生幽泉。朝日艷且鮮。秋花冒綠水。密葉羅青
煙。秀色空絕世。馨香竟誰傳。坐看飛霜滿。凋此紅
芳年。結根未得所。願託華池邊。

六三、寄 東 魯 二 稚 子

吳地桑葉綠。吳蠶已三眠。我家寄東魯。誰種龜陰

田。春事已不及。江行復茫然。南風吹歸心。飛墮酒
樓前。樓東一株桃。枝葉拂青煙。此樹我所種。別來
向三年。桃今與樓齊。我行尙未旋。嬌女字平陽。折
花倚桃邊。折花不見我。淚下如流泉。小兒名伯禽。
與姊亦齊肩。雙行桃樹下。撫背復誰憐。念此失次
第。肝腸日憂煎。裂素寫遠意。因之汶陽川。

六四、送蕭三十一之魯中兼問稚子伯禽

六月南風吹白沙。吳牛喘月氣成霞。水國鬱蒸不可
處。時炎道遠無行車。夫子如何涉江路。雲帆裊裊
金陵去。高堂倚門望伯魚。魯中正是趨庭處。我家
寄左沙丘旁。三年不歸空斷腸。君行旣識伯禽子。
應駕小車騎白羊。

六五、友人會宿

滌蕩千古愁。留連百壺飲。良宵宜淸談。皓月未能
寢。醉來臥空山。天地卽衾枕。

六六、擬　古

生者爲過客。死者爲歸人。天地一逆旅。同悲萬古。

塵。月兔空擣藥。扶桑已成薪　白骨寂無言。靑松豈
知春。前後更嘆息。浮榮何足珍。

六七、雙燕離

雙燕復雙燕。雙飛令人羨。玉樓珠閣不獨棲。金窓
繡戶長相見。栢梁失火去。雙雌憶故雄。雙飛難
再得。傷我寸心中。雙飛庶集亦空。憔悴一身在。
蕩。雛盡巢亦空。憔悴一身在。翩翩憶故雄。雙飛難
釣磯。

六八、送客歸吳

江村秋雨歇。酒盡一帆飛。路歷波濤去。家惟坐臥
歸。島花開灼灼。汀柳綱依依。別後無餘事。還應掃
釣磯。

六九、自代內贈

妾似井底桃。開花向誰笑。君如天上月。不肯一廻
照。竇刀裁流水。無有斷絕時。妾意逐君行。綢繆亦如
之。

七〇、荊州歌

白帝城邊足風波。瞿塘五月誰敢過。荊州麥熟繭成蛾。繰絲憶君頭緒多。撥穀飛鳴奈妾何。

七一、古風

莊周夢蝴蝶。蝴蝶為莊周。一體更變易。萬事良悠悠。乃知蓬萊水。復作清淺流。青門種瓜人。昔日東陵侯。富貴故如此。營營何所求。

七二、哭晁卿行

日本晁卿辭帝都。征帆一片繞蓬壺。明月不歸沈碧海。白雲愁色滿蒼梧。

七三、江南春懷

青春幾何時。黃鳥鳴不歇。天涯失鄉路。江外老華髮。心飛秦塞雲。影滯楚關月。身世殊爛漫。田園久蕪沒。歲晏何所從。長歌謝金闕。

七四、蜀道難

噫吁戲危乎高哉。蜀道之難難於上青天。蠶叢及魚鳧。開國何茫然。爾來四萬八千歲。不與秦塞通人煙。西當太白有鳥道。可以橫絕峨眉巔。地崩山摧壯士死。然後天梯石棧相鉤連。上有六龍回日之高標。下有衝波逆折之回川。黃鶴之飛尚不得過。猿猱欲度愁攀援。青泥何盤盤。百步九折縈巖巒。捫參歷井仰脅息。以手撫膺坐長歎。問君西遊何時還。畏途巉巖不可攀。但見悲鳥號古木。雄飛雌從繞林間。又聞子規啼夜月愁空山。蜀道之難難於上青天。使人聽此凋朱顏。連峰去天不盈尺。枯松倒挂倚絕壁。飛湍瀑流爭喧豗。砯崖轉石萬壑雷。其險也如此。嗟爾遠道之人胡為乎來哉。劍閣崢嶸而崔嵬。一夫當關萬夫莫開。所守或匪親。化為狼與豺。朝避猛虎。夕避長蛇。磨牙吮血殺人如麻。錦城雖云樂。不如早還家。蜀道之難難於上青天。側身西望長咨嗟。

七五、金陵酒肆留別

風吹柳花滿店香。吳姬壓酒使客嘗。金陵子弟來相送。欲行不行各盡觴。請君試問東流水。別意與之誰短長。

七六、登金陵鳳凰臺

鳳凰臺上鳳凰遊。鳳去臺空江自流。吳宮花草埋幽
徑。晉代衣冠成古丘。三山半落青天外。二水中分
白鷺洲。總爲浮雲能蔽日。長安不見使人愁。

七七、夢遊天姥吟留別

海客談瀛洲。煙濤微茫信難求。越人語天姥。雲霞
明滅或可覩。天姥連天向天橫。勢拔五嶽掩赤城。
天台四萬八千丈。對此欲倒東南傾。我欲因之夢吳
越。一夜飛度鏡湖月。湖月照我影。送我至剡溪。謝
公宿處今尚在。淥水蕩漾清猿啼。腳著謝公屐。身
登青雲梯。半壁見海日。空中聞天雞。千巖萬轉路
不定。迷花倚石忽已暝。熊咆龍吟殷巖泉。慄深林
兮驚層巔。雲青青兮欲雨。水澹澹兮生烟。列缺霹
靂。丘巒崩摧。洞天石扉。訇然中開。青冥浩蕩不見
底。日月照耀金銀臺。霓爲衣兮風爲馬。雲之君兮
紛紛而來下。虎鼓瑟兮鸞回車。僊之人兮列如麻。
忽魂悸以魄動。怳驚起而長嗟。惟覺時之枕席。失

向來之煙霞。世間行樂亦如此。古來萬事東流水。
別君去兮何時還。且放白鹿青崖間。須行即騎訪名
山。安能摧眉折腰事權貴。使我不得開心顏。

七八、對酒憶賀監

四明有狂客。風流賀季眞。長安一相見。呼我謫仙
人。昔好杯中物。翻爲松下塵。金龜換酒處。却憶淚
沾巾。

七九、南陵別兒童入京

白酒新熟山中歸。黃雞啄黍秋正肥。呼童烹雞酌白
酒。兒女嬉笑牽人衣。高歌取醉欲自慰。起舞落日
爭光輝。游說萬乘苦不早。著鞭跨馬涉遠道。會稽
愚婦輕買臣。余亦辭家西入秦。仰天大笑出門去。
我輩豈是蓬蒿人。

八〇、沙丘城下寄杜甫

我來竟何事。高臥沙丘城。城邊有古樹。日夕連秋
聲。魯酒不可醉。齊歌空復情。思君若汶水。浩蕩寄
南征。

八一、月下獨酌

天若不愛酒。酒星不在天。地若不愛酒。地應無酒
泉。天地既愛酒。愛酒不愧天。已聞清比聖。復道濁
如賢。賢聖既已飲。何必求神仙。三杯通大道。一斗
合自然。但得酒中趣。勿爲醒者傳。

八二、贈盧門戶

秋色無遠近。出門盡寒山。白雲遙相識。待我蒼梧
間。借問盧耽鶴。西飛幾歲還。

八三、沐浴子

沐芳莫彈冠。浴蘭莫振衣。處世忌太潔。至人貴藏
暉。滄浪有釣叟。吾與爾同歸。

八四、見京兆韋參軍量移東陽

潮水還歸海。流人却到吳。相逢問愁苦。淚盡日南
珠。

八五、採蓮曲

若耶溪傍採蓮女。笑隔荷花共人語。日照新妝水底

明。風飄香袂空中舉。岸上誰家遊冶郎。三三五五
映垂楊。紫騮嘶入落花去。見此踟躕空斷腸。

八六、君馬黃

君馬黃我馬白。馬色雖不同。人心本無隔。共作遊
冶盤。雙行洛陽陌。長劍旣照曜。高冠何赩赫。各有
千金裘。俱爲五侯客。猛虎落陷穽。壯夫時屈厄。相
知在急難。獨好亦何益。

八七、白紵辭

揚清歌。發皓齒。北方佳人東鄰子。且吟白紵停綠
水。長袖拂面爲君起。寒雲夜卷霜海空。胡風吹天
飄塞鴻。玉顏滿堂樂未終。館娃日落歌吹濃。

八八、俠客行

趙客縵胡纓。吳鉤霜雪明。銀鞍照白馬。颯沓如流
星。十步殺一人。千里不留行。事了拂衣去。深藏身
與名。閑過信陵飲。脫劍膝前橫。將炙啖朱亥。持觴
勸侯嬴。三杯吐然諾。五嶽倒爲輕。眼花耳熱後。意

[12]

氣素寬生。救趙揮金槌。邯鄲先震驚。千秋二壯士。
烜赫大梁城。縱使俠骨香。不慚世上英。惟能書閣
下。白首太玄經。

八九、江夏贈常南陵氷

胡驕馬驚沙塵起。胡雛飲馬天津水。君爲張掖近酒
泉。我竄三巴九千里。天地再新法令寬。夜郎遷客
帶霜寒。西憶故人不可見。東風吹夢到長安。寧期
此地忽相遇。驚喜茫如墮煙霧。玉簫金管喧四筵。
苦心不得申長句。昨日繡衣傾綠樽。病如桃李竟何
言。昔騎天子大宛馬。今乘欵段諸侯門。遇遇南平
絡方寸。復兼夫子持清論。有似山開萬里雲。四望
青天解人間。人間還心悶。苦辛長苦辛。愁來飲酒
二千石。寒灰重暖生陽春。山公醉後能騎馬。別是
風流賢主人。頭陀雲月多僧氣。山水何曾稱人意。
不然鳴笳按鼓戲滄流。呼取江南女兒歌櫂謳。我且
爲君槌碎黃鶴樓。君亦爲吾倒却鸚鵡洲。赤壁爭雄
如夢裏。且須歌舞寬離憂。

九〇、望廬山瀑布水 一

西登香爐峰。南見瀑布水。挂流三百丈。噴壑數十
里。欻如飛電來。隱若白虹起。初驚河漢落。半灑雲
天裏。仰觀勢轉雄。壯哉造化功。海風吹不斷。江月
照還空。空中亂潈射。左右洗青壁。飛珠散輕霞。流
沫沸穹石。而我樂名山。對之心益閑。無論漱瓊液。
還得洗塵顏。且諧宿所好。永願辭人間。

九一、望廬山瀑布水 二

日照香爐生紫煙。遙看瀑布挂長川。飛流直下三千
尺。疑是銀河落九天。

九二、遠別離

遠別離。古有皇英之二女。乃在洞庭之南。瀟湘之
浦。海水直下萬里深。誰人不言此離苦。日慘慘兮
雲冥冥。猩猩啼煙兮鬼嘯雨。我縱言之將何補。皇
穹竊恐不照余之忠誠。雲憑憑兮欲吼怒。堯舜當之
亦禪禹。君失臣兮龍爲魚。權歸臣兮鼠變虎。或言
堯幽囚舜野死。九疑聯綿皆相似。重瞳孤墳竟何

是。帝子泣兮綠雲間。隨風波兮去無還。慟哭兮遠望。見蒼梧之深山。蒼梧山崩湘水絕。竹上之淚乃可滅。

九三、王昭君一

昭君拂玉鞍。上馬啼紅頰。今日漢宮人。明朝胡地妾。

九四、王昭君二

漢家秦地月。流影送明妃。一上玉關道。天涯去不歸。漢月還從東海出。明妃西嫁無來日。燕支長寒雪作花。蛾眉憔悴沒胡沙。生乏黃金枉圖畫。死留青塚使人嗟。

九五、北風行

燭龍棲寒門。光曜猶旦開。日月照之何不及此。唯有北風號怒天上來。燕山雪花大如席。片片吹落軒轅臺。幽州思婦十二月。停歌罷笑雙蛾摧。倚門望行人。念君長城苦寒良可哀。別時提劍救邊去。遺此虎紋金鞞靫。中有一雙白羽箭。蜘蛛結網生塵埃。

箭空在。人今戰死不復回。不忍見此物。焚之已成灰。黃河捧土尚可塞。北風雨雪恨難裁。

九六、關山月

明月出天山。蒼茫雲海間。長風幾萬里。吹度玉門關。漢下白登道。胡窺青海灣。由來征戰地。不見有人還。戍客望邊色。思歸多苦顏。高樓當此夜。歎息未應閑。

九七、戰城南

去年戰桑乾源。今年戰蔥河道。洗兵條支海上波。放馬天山雪中草。萬里長征戰。三軍盡衰老。匈奴以殺戮為耕作。古來唯見白骨黃沙田。秦家築城備胡處。漢家還有烽火燃。烽火然不息。征戰無已時。野戰格鬥死。敗馬號鳴向天悲。烏鳶啄人腸。銜飛上掛枯樹枝。士卒塗草莽。將軍空爾為。乃知兵者是凶器。聖人不得已而用之。

九八、前有樽酒行

春風東來忽相過。金樽淥酒生微波。落花紛紛稍覺

多。美人欲醉朱顏酡。青軒桃李能幾何。流光欺人
忽蹉跎。君起舞。日西夕。當年意氣不肯平。白髮如
絲歎何益。

九九、題元丹丘山居

故人棲東山。自愛丘壑美。青春臥空林。白日猶不
起。松風清襟袖。石潭洗心耳。羨君無紛喧。高枕碧
霞裏。

一〇〇、三五七言

秋風清。秋月明。落葉聚還散。寒鴉棲復驚。相思相
見知何日。此時此夜難爲情。

一〇一、子夜春歌

秦地羅敷女。採桑綠水邊。素手青條上。紅粧白日
鮮。蠶飢妾欲去。五馬莫留連。

一〇二、子夜夏歌

鏡湖三百里。菡萏發荷花。五月西施採。人看隘若
耶。回舟不待月。歸去越王家。

一〇三、子夜吳歌

長安一片月。萬戶擣衣聲。秋風吹不盡。總是玉關
情。何日平胡虜。良人罷遠征。

一〇四、子夜冬歌

明日驛使發。一夜絮征袍。素手抽針冷。那堪把剪
刀。裁縫寄遠道。幾日到臨洮。

一〇五、長 于 行 一

妾髮初覆額。折花門前劇。郎騎竹馬來。遶牀弄青
梅。同居長干里。兩小無嫌猜。十四爲君婦。羞顏未
嘗開。低頭向暗壁。千喚不一廻。十五始展眉。願同
塵與灰。常存抱柱信。豈上望夫臺。十六君遠行。瞿
塘灩澦堆。五月不可觸。猿聲天上哀。門前遲行跡。
一一生綠苔。苔深不能掃。落葉秋風早。八月蝴蝶
黃。雙飛西園草。感此傷妾心。坐愁紅顏老。早晚下
三巴。預將書報家。相迎不道遠。直至長風沙。

一〇六、長 于 行 二

憶妾深閨裏。烟塵不曾識。嫁與長干人。沙頭候風

色。五月南風興。思君下巴陵。八月西風起。想君發揚子。去來悲如何。見少別離多。湘潭幾月刻。妾夢越風波。昨夜狂風度。吹折江頭樹。淼淼暗無邊。行人在何處。好乘浮雲驄。佳期蘭渚東。鴛鴦綠蒲上。翡翠金屏中。自憐十五餘。顏色挑花紅。那作商人婦。愁水復愁風。

一〇七、登新平樓

去國登茲樓。懷歸傷暮秋。天長落日遠。水淨寒波流。秦雲起嶺樹。胡雁飛沙洲。蒼蒼幾萬里。目極令人愁。

一〇八、訪戴天山道士不遇

犬吠水聲中。桃花帶露濃。樹深時見鹿。溪午不聞鐘。野竹分青靄。飛泉挂碧峰。無人知所去。愁倚兩三松。

一〇九、尋山僧不遇作

石徑入丹壑。松門閉青苔。閑階有鳥跡。禪室無人閉。窺窗見白拂。挂壁生塵埃。使我空歎息。欲去仍徘徊。香雲偏山起。花雨從天來。已有空樂好。況聞青猿哀。了然絕世事。此地方悠哉。

一一〇、望月有懷

清泉映疏松。不知幾千古。寒月搖清波。流光入窗戶。對此空長吟。思君意何深。無因見安道。興盡愁人心。

一一一、尋高鳳石門山中元丹丘

尋幽無前期。乘興不覺遠。蒼崖渺難涉。白日忽欲晚。未窮三四山。已歷千萬轉。寂寂聞猿愁。行行見雲收。高松來好月。空谷宜清秋。溪深古雪在。石斷寒泉流。峰巒秀中天。登眺不可盡。丹丘遙相呼。顧我忽而哂。遂造窮谷間。始知靜者閑。留歡達永夜。清曉方言還。

一一二、送殷淑

痛飲龍筇下。燈青月復寒。醉歌驚白鷺。半夜起沙灘。

一一三、廬山謠寄盧侍御盧舟

我本楚狂人。鳳歌笑孔丘。手持綠玉杖。朝別黃鶴
樓。五嶽尋仙不辭遠。一生好入名山遊。廬山秀出
南斗傍。屏風九疊雲錦張。影落明湖青黛光。金闕
前開二峰長。銀河倒挂三石梁。香爐瀑布遙相望。
迴崖沓嶂凌蒼蒼。翠影紅霞映朝日。鳥飛不到吳天
長。登高壯觀天地間。大江茫茫去不還。黃雲萬里
動風色。白波九道流雪山。好爲廬山謠。興因廬山
發。閒窺石鏡清我心。謝公行處蒼苔沒。早服還丹
無世情。琴心三疊道初成。遙見仙人綵雲裏。手把
芙蓉朝玉京。先期汗漫九垓上。願接盧放遊太清。

一一四、別內赴徵 一

王命三徵去未還。明朝離別出吳關。白玉高樓看不
見。相思須上望夫山。

一一五、別內赴徵 二

出門妻子強牽衣。問我西行幾日歸。歸時儻珮黃金
印。莫學蘇秦不下機。

一一六、別內赴徵 三

翡翠爲樓金作梯。誰人獨宿倚門啼。夜坐寒燈連曉
月。行行淚盡楚關西。

一一七、秋浦吟

白髮三千丈。緣愁似箇長。不知明鏡裏。何處得秋
霜。

一一八、流夜郎贈辛判官

昔在長安醉花柳。五侯七貴同杯酒。氣岸遙凌豪士
前。風流肯落他人後。夫子紅顏我少年。章臺走馬
著金鞭。文章獻納麒麟殿。歌舞淹留玳瑁筵。與君
自謂長如此。寧知草動風塵起。函谷忽驚胡馬來。
秦宮桃李向明開。我愁遠謫夜郎去。何日金雞放赦
回。

一一九、與史郎中欽聽黃鶴樓上吹笛

一爲遷客去長沙。西望長安不見家。黃鶴樓中吹玉
笛。江城五月落梅花。

一二〇、春夜洛城聞笛

誰家玉笛暗飛聲。散入春風滿洛城。此夜曲中聞折
柳。何人不起故園情。

一二一、陪族叔刑部侍郎曄及中
書賈舍人至。遊洞庭。一
洞庭西望楚江分。水盡南天不見雲。日落長沙秋色
遠。不知何處弔湘君。

一二二、陪族叔刑部侍郎曄。及中
書賈舍人至。遊洞庭。二
南湖秋水夜無煙。耐可乘流直上天。且就洞庭賒月
色。將船買酒白雲邊。

一二三、南流夜郎寄內
夜郎天外怨離居。明月樓中音信疎。北雁春歸看欲
盡。南來不得豫章書。

一二四、經亂離後。天恩流夜郎。憶舊
遊書懷。贈江夏韋太守良宰。
天上白玉京。十二樓五城。仙人撫我頂。結髮受長

生。誤逐世間樂。顏窮理亂情。九十六聖君。浮雲掛
空名。天地賭一擲。未能忘戰爭。試涉霸王略。將期
軒冕榮。時命乃大謬。棄之海上行。學劍翻自哂。爲
文竟何成。劍非萬人敵。文竊四海聲。兒戲不足道。爲
五噫出西京。臨當欲去時。慷慨淚沾纓。歎君偶儻
才。標舉冠群英。開筵引祖帳。慰此遠祖征。鞍馬若
浮雲。送余驃騎亭。歌鐘不盡意。白日落昆明。十月
到幽州。戈鋋若羅星。君王棄北海。掃地借長鯨。呼
吸走百川。燕然可摧傾。心知不得語。却欲樓蓬瀛。
彎弧懼天狼。挾矢不敢張。擁涕黃金臺。呼天哭昭
王。無人貴駿骨。綠耳空騰驤。樂毅儻再生。於今亦
奔亡。蹉跎不得意。驅馬還貴鄉。逢君聽絃歌。肅穆
坐華堂。百里獨太古。陶然臥羲皇。徵樂昌樂舘。開
筵列壺觴。賢豪間青娥。對燭儼成行。醉舞紛綺席。
清歌繞飛梁。歡娛未終朝。秋滿歸咸陽。祖道擁萬
人。供帳逶相望。一別隔千里。榮枯異炎涼。炎涼幾
度改。九土中橫潰。漢甲連胡兵。沙塵暗雲海。草木
搖殺氣。星辰無光彩。白骨成丘山。蒼生竟何罪。函

關壯帝居。國命懸哥舒。長戟三十萬。開門納兇渠。公卿如犬羊。忠讜醢與葅。二聖出遊豫。兩京遂丘墟。帝子許專征。秉旄控彊楚。節制非桓文。軍師擁熊虎。人心失去就。賊勢騰風雨。惟君固房陵。誠節冠終古。僕臥香爐頂。餐霞漱瑤泉。門開九江轉。枕下五湖連。半夜水軍來。潯陽滿旌旃。空名適自誤。迫脅上樓船。徒賜五百金。棄之若浮煙。辭官不受賞。翻謫夜郎天。夜郎萬里道。西上令人老。掃蕩六合清。仍為負霜草。日月無偏照。何由訴蒼天。良牧稱神明。深仁恤交道。一忝青雲客。三登黃鶴樓。顧慚禰處士。虛對鸚鵡洲。樊山霸氣盡。寥落天地秋。江帶峨眉雪。川橫三峽流。萬舸此中來。連帆過楊州。送此萬里目。曠然散我愁。紗忽倚天開。木樹綠如髮。窺日長衛山。促酒喜得月。吳娃與越豔。窈窕誇鉛紅。呼來上雲梯。含笑出簾櫳。對客小垂手。羅衣舞春風。賓跪請休息。主人情未極。覽君荊山作。江豹堆動色。清水出芙蓉。天然去雕飾。逸興橫素襟。無時不招尋。朱門擁虎士。列戟何森森。剪繁竹

石開。縈流濊清深。登樓坐水閣。吐論多英音。片辭貴白璧。一諾輕黃金。謂我不愧君。青鳥明丹心。五色雲間鵲。飛鳴天上來。傳閱敕書至。卻放夜郎迴。暖氣變寒谷。炎烟生死灰。君登鳳池去。忽棄賈生才。縱犬卻吠堯。匈奴笑千秋。中夜四五歎。常為大國憂。旌旆夾兩山。黃河當中流。連雞不得進。飲馬空夷猶。安得羿善射。一箭落旄頭。

一二五、飲中八仙歌　杜甫

知章騎馬似乘船。眼花落井水底眠。汝陽三斗始朝天。道逢麴車口流涎。恨不移封向酒泉。左相日興費萬錢。飲如長鯨吸百川。銜杯樂聖稱避賢。宗之瀟灑美少年。舉觴白眼望青天。皎如玉樹臨風前。蘇晉長齋繡佛前。醉中往往愛逃禪。李白一斗詩百篇。長安市上酒家眠。天子呼來不上船。自稱臣是酒中仙。張旭三杯草聖傳。脫帽露頂王公前。揮毫落紙如雲煙。焦遂五斗方卓然。高談雄辯驚四筵。

一二六、天寶五載初罷相作 李適之

避賢初罷相。樂聖且銜杯。爲問門前客。今朝幾箇
來。

一二七、與李十二同尋范十隱居 杜甫

李侯有佳句。往往似陰鏗。余亦東蒙客。憐君如弟
兄。醉眠秋共被。攜手日同行。更想幽期處。還尋北
郭生。入門高興發。侍立小童清。落景開寒杵。屯雲
對古城。向來吟橘頌。誰欲討蓴羹。不顧論簪笏。悠
悠滄海情。

一二八、洞庭送李十二赴零陵 賈至

今日相逢落葉前。洞庭秋水遠連天。共說金華舊遊
處。迴看北斗欲潸然。

一二九、贈李十二 崔宗之

凉秋八九月。白露空園亭。耿耿意不暢。梢梢風葉
聲。想見雄俊士。共語今古情。李侯忽來儀。把袂苦
不早。清論旣抵掌。玄談又絕倒。分明楚漢事。歷歷

王霸道。擔囊無俗物。訪古千里餘。袖有七首劍。懷
中茂陵書。雙眸光照人。詞賦凌子虛。酌酒絃素琴。
霜氣正凝潔。平生心中事。今日爲君說。清淡澄素光。雲散窻
戶靜。風吹松桂香。子若同斯游。千載不相忘。

一三〇、春日憶李白 杜甫

白也詩無敵。飄然思不群。清新庾開府。俊逸鮑參
軍。渭北春天樹。江東日暮雲。何時一尊酒。重與細
論文。

一三一、不見 近無李白消息 杜甫

不見李生久。佯狂眞可憐。世人皆欲殺。吾意獨憐
才。敏捷詩千首。飄零酒一盃。匡山讀書處。頭白好
歸來。

一三二、李白之墓 白居易

采石江邊李白墳。遶田無限草連雲。可憐荒隴窮泉
骨。曾有驚天動地文。但是詩人多薄命。就中淪落
不遇君。